KICK THE HABIT

D0433031

HOW TO **STOP**
SMOKING
AND **STAY STOPPED**

ABOUT THE AUTHOR

In 1974 Martin Raw joined the Maudsley Smokers Clinic in south London to develop and research new treatment methods for smokers. Over the next few years he pioneered the use of nicotine chewing gum in stop smoking groups at the clinic, and he was one of the authors of the first scientific study which proved that the gum worked. He gained his doctorate on methods to help smokers stop. In 1983 he published a report recommending that smokers' clinics should be offered through the National Health Service, a recommendation finally put into practice at the end of the 1990s. He has run groups to help smokers stop for over 25 years.

He is co-author of *Clearing the Air: A guide for action on tobacco*, published in 1990, and of a 1993 training course for nurses and other health professionals. He was deputy editor of the international scientific journal *Addiction* from 1989–95 and has published over a hundred reports, articles and booklets on the subject. He holds an honorary senior lectureship in public health at the University of London, and leads a project for the World Health Organization on the development of treatment for smokers throughout Europe. He has written numerous guides and booklets for smokers on how to stop, but this is the first time he has combined his scientific knowledge and clinical experience in a popular paperback for smokers.

HOW TO **STOP**
SMOKING
AND **STAY STOPPED**

Martin Raw

This book is published to accompany BBC Education's *Kick the Habit* health campaign first broadcast on BBC ONE, BBC TWO, BBC Radio 2 and BBC Radio 4 in March 2000

Commissioning Executive for BBC Education: Jill Pack
Project Manager: Mark Duman

Published by BBC Worldwide Ltd,
Woodlands, 80 Wood Lane, London W12 0TT
First published 2000

ISBN 0 563 55185 2

Commissioning Editor: Viv Bowler
Project Editor: Martha Caute
Text Editor: Sue Tucker
Designer: Ben Cracknell

Set in Palatino and Gill by BBC Worldwide Ltd
Printed and bound in Great Britain by Martins the Printers Ltd,
Berwick-upon-Tweed.
Cover printed by Belmont Press Ltd, Northampton

CONTENTS

DEDICATION

This book is dedicated to Richard Gillette, Michael Russell and Ove Ferno, who set me on my journey.

INTRODUCTION

A journey of a thousand miles begins with a single step
Chinese proverb

It was over 25 years ago that I was taken on to develop the treatment and research programme at the Maudsley Smokers Clinic in south London. Our goal was to find more effective ways to help smokers stop and I arrived at the clinic just as nicotine chewing gum was being developed. In those early years we tested the gum and we were the first team in the world to demonstrate that it worked. We also refined group methods to help smokers stop. The hallmark of our approach was (and remains) the combination of the two key aspects of smoking: the physical addiction and the psychological habit. Scientific research has since confirmed that smoking is not only a habit but also an addiction, and the methods we pioneered at the clinic have stood the test of time.

The approach used in this book has grown directly from my work over these 25 years, from the scientific research on treatment methods, of course, but more importantly from the smokers themselves. I have lost count of how many groups I have run in that time or how many smokers I have seen. But I have learned from them all. It is their experience as well as mine that you can now draw on to help you stop. Many thousands of them have been down this road before you and succeeded in stopping.

In this book I will take you through the stages of stopping smoking. I will help you make up your mind, prepare a plan, stop and then stay stopped. I will answer your questions and explain what we know about the addictiveness of smoking, and why it is so dangerous. I also provide the latest details of the nicotine replacement therapies and how they work. Finally, many ex-smokers were interviewed and I have included their experiences – in their own words – in this book. They have stopped smoking: you can too.

THINKING ABOUT
STOPPING

PREPARING TO
STOP

STOPPING

STAYING
STOPPED

Some smokers wake up one morning and think, without any warning or preparation at all, 'Right. That's it. I'm not smoking any more'. and stop right then, for good, the first time they ever tried. But not many. Research suggests that on average, smokers try to stop three or four times before eventually succeeding. They learn from each attempt, until finally everything comes together and they make it. In other words, most smokers go through a process when they try to stop, and for most, the process does not happen overnight. It takes time.

Of course, this is not a rigid rule and there are exceptions: everyone is different and will arrive at their destination by different routes. However, there are two key principles to stopping. These form the basis of the approach in this book and apply to all smokers.

TWO KEY PRINCIPLES

The first principle is that stopping smoking is a process. Just because you did not manage to stay stopped once before does not mean you have failed. Stopping smoking is a learning process which may be quick or may take several attempts but which will, if you allow it, eventually end in success. So, there's no need to feel guilty if you don't stop the first time. It is your process, not someone else's, and ultimately you owe it only to yourself to stop – if, of course, that is what you really want.

This leads me to the second principle. This is that stopping smoking is a choice. The first part of the process of stopping – and the most important – is deciding if you want to stop. Ask yourself 'What do I really want?' If you want to stop, you can choose to. I am not saying it will be easy (although it might be). I am not saying that smoking is 'just a habit' (even if it is a very strong one). Smoking is an addiction, rated by some scientists as one of the most powerful of all the addictions (see **More facts about smoking**, p. 101). But it is an addiction which can be beaten if you want to beat it.

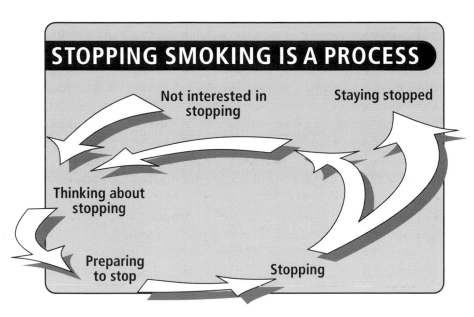

Once you have decided that you want to stop, the rest is detail (although admittedly important detail). It might be easy, it might be difficult, but it is detail. This chapter is about making that choice. By the end of the chapter you will be ready to start preparing your stop smoking plan. In fact, I urge you not to try to do anything until you have completed this chapter and decided you are ready for change.

STARTING
THE PROCESS

You may not be able to identify exactly when the process started. It could have been years, months, days or minutes ago. It may have started with the rumblings of a chesty cough that won't quite go away as quickly as it used to. Maybe something someone said, something you read or saw or something that happened – possibly someone else's illness – started you thinking. Or you may have gradually become aware that you are unhappy being a smoker, and are contemplating

SPENCER · 25

'I started smoking at the age of 13 (as does everyone, I think, who starts smoking young). I didn't see it as that bad. My father smoked a lot and when my parents split up I just thought it was a grown-up thing to do. I guess that's what all 13-year-olds think when they start smoking. I decided to give up last year for a number of reasons. I was no longer enjoying it. I found it more and more difficult to fit cigarettes into a busy day at work and the smell and the wheezing at the top of the stairs, etc. The final thing that did it was that I was ill and suffering chest pains. One day I went to get off the sofa and I thought I was having a heart attack. Extreme pain. So I went to the doctor, had blood tests done and nothing was wrong with me. So I decided to give up smoking. It was easier than I expected. The first two weeks were tough (chewing nicotine gum) but after that things got slightly better and I didn't need any aids.'

something that was once unthinkable – stopping. This chapter will help you make up your mind that you are ready for change. After you have done that the rest will be much easier. Most of it is applied common sense: preparation, good planning and getting help.

THOUGHTS INTO ACTION

Now you've started to read about stopping smoking, you might also talk to other people and collect more information. Then you start to think about actually having a go yourself – changing your behaviour.

IAN · 51

'I had my first cigarette at about 13 when it was a big, brave thing to do with some mates. But I suppose I started smoking when I was 16, actually having my own cigarettes. When I was at college, I smoked about 30 a day, when it was sort of exam stress. That was my maximum. I stopped just the once. January 3rd. Why? Last summer I was on holiday, and I was doing my usual scuba diving and finding that I was letting people down by using my air up rather quickly and being somewhat breathless and wheezy and what have you. Frankly I was not able to do as much as I wanted to and it had to be the smoking. So I thought I will give up smoking. There was also pressure from the family (had been for years) – the fact that it wasn't healthy. Failing at the scuba diving was the final bit of the jigsaw, if you like. I went diving again this summer and I found I was able to cope with it much better. Even after 10 months my chest has now cleared. I won't go into details but it wasn't very pleasant the first few months what was being brought up from my lungs. I certainly feel fitter. I put on 11lbs in weight but I've lost 8lbs of it now. There was only one difficult moment, when I felt like punching someone's face. But I gritted my teeth, turned my back and walked away.'

You think about it, you plan it, then you do it. Think of it as going through a kind of revolving door. At first you are outside the door. This is what some experts have called a 'contented smoker.' This is someone who is happy smoking or is not considering stopping. There are fewer and fewer of these smokers around. Once you step into the revolving door you have begun the process of change. You might just go round the circle and straight out, or you might go round several times before coming out the other side a non-smoker. The chances are that you already have been round several times and are now ready for a final spin.

The icing on the cake is that once you've changed your behaviour, your self-image will also gradually change. You'll begin to think of yourself as a non-smoker. It happens after your body has got rid of the toxic chemicals from tobacco smoke, and the desire for a cigarette has faded. It takes time but it is great when it happens. This is how Vicky, 24, described it: 'Three months was a big turning point for me. I suddenly realized that I was going two or three days without thinking about it.'

MAKING UP YOUR MIND

Now, there are smokers who have had enough of smoking, hate it, no longer get any enjoyment out of it, who are just addicted to the nicotine and are ready to stop. If this is you, you can skip the rest of this chapter and go straight to **Stage 2: Preparing to stop**, p. 30. If not, you need to ask yourself the question 'Do I really want to stop?'

Do you? There are no prizes for putting yourself through stopping smoking if you are not sure you want to, or if you are not ready. There are no prizes for suffering. If you are human, the answer to the question is probably 'yes and no.' What you are going to check now is that it is more 'yes' than 'no'.

I want to emphasize at this stage that honesty is the best policy. There is no point in trying to persuade yourself you ought to stop, or trying to pretend you want to. You won't get there by trying to believe what you ought to believe, or what other people think you should believe. Once you know what you really feel then you will be in a position to move forward.

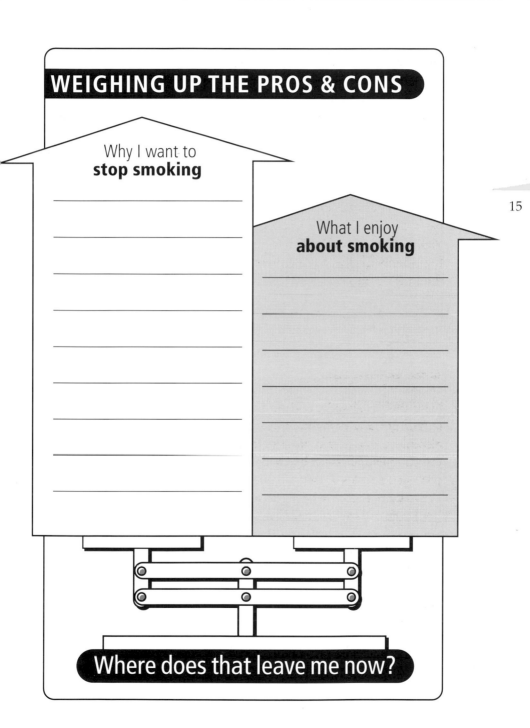

WEIGHING UP THE PROS & CONS

Why I want to **stop smoking**

What I enjoy **about smoking**

Where does that leave me now?

ROBIN · 61

'It was all the publicity really that made me decide that I had to give up. Seeing television programmes, and knowing that heart attacks are a direct cause. I'm at the age where I really should be looking after myself. I just decided one day that I'd had enough. I didn't tell anyone, I think that some people can get away with doing it secretly rather than tell the family, when they'll all try to urge me on and remind me. I just gave it up in one fell swoop and I haven't smoked since.'

Fill in the two sides of the scales in the 'Weighing up the pros & cons' chart. Take your time. Think about it. If you need some more facts about smoking there are plenty in the rest of the book and especially in **More facts about smoking**, p.101, including information about just how dangerous it really is. But the health risks are only one aspect of smoking and there may be other things that are important for you. The really important thing is for you to explore what you feel. Do you know how dangerous smoking is? Do you think you are at risk? Do you care? What other factors are important for you? When you have filled in the two columns, you need to ask yourself 'Where does that leave me now?'

This will help you clarify what you really want to do. If you are not interested in stopping, all you really need to do now is remember why you picked up this book in the first place and either put it on your shelf until the next time you are thinking about stopping, lend it to a friend, or read the last chapter. If you are interested in stopping but need more time to think about it and prepare then carry on reading this chapter. If you are ready to stop you can go straight to **Stage 2: Preparing to stop**, p.30.

WHERE ARE YOU NOW?

You now have a list of reasons for wanting to stop smoking and possibly some reasons you want to continue smoking. Before continuing, ask yourself: 'Are the reasons for stopping more important to me than the things I enjoy about smoking?'

Weighing up the pros and cons is an exercise in honesty as much as anything else, because you might as well admit it if there are things about smoking you will miss. Then you can plan how to cope. As you go through this book you will learn how to live without them, or how to replace them where that is possible. You may have to accept that there are some things about smoking you will just learn to do without. Being open about the cons as well as the pros means being able to face them and being able to deal with them. It means not being surprised by something you were not aware of. Forewarned is forearmed.

COSTAS · 54

'It was nearly three years ago in January. It was after an illness and I was feeling terrible, headaches. My wife and sons were on to me. They said it was killing them and it was killing me. That was it. It had to go. I tried once before for more than six months. I used to smoke 2oz a week, then it went up to 2oz a day before I gave up. It was burning money like crazy and the tobacco was getting more and more expensive plus I couldn't smoke in public places or where I work (I work in the building trade). I work with a lot of rich people and they didn't like smoking so there was no point in taking a pipe.'

WHAT WOULD YOU REALLY BE
GOING WITHOUT?

There is remarkably little scientific evidence that smoking has any benefits. It is possible that the nicotine helps some smokers concentrate, but there are much safer stimulants, coffee for example, and much safer ways of getting nicotine if you must have it. Many smokers feel that smoking helps them cope with stress but the reasons for this are more to do with addiction and withdrawal, than with the properties of nicotine or tobacco smoke. In fact, new research suggests that smokers as a group are more stressed than non-smokers and ex-smokers, not less stressed. In other words, smoking itself increases anxiety and stress levels. This makes sense since nicotine is a stimulant not a tranquillizer.

In any case, even if smoking did help you cope with stress it would be a remarkably dangerous coping mechanism, since it is one which will very possibly kill you. If you want to stop you'll have to find better ways of coping, and we'll come to that later. On the chart opposite write down any more reasons that are important to you. You can add to the list at any time and will find it useful in the coming weeks to be able to refer back to it. Everyone needs a reason to give up. What's yours?

ARM YOURSELF
WITH THE FACTS

It is human to judge risk according to our own experiences, values, prejudices and hopes. What else can we do? But it's no bad thing sometimes to have the facts to inform our judgements. You can always ignore them if you want to, but at least if you have them you have the option of using them. I have already explained that in the end you must make your own decision and no amount of facts or statistics will force you to go down a path you don't want to go down. Smokers who say 'Yes but my granny smoked 30 a day and lived to 90' or

MORE REASONS TO STOP

- ○ I want to be healthy
- ○ I don't want my children to become smokers
- ○ It's not fair to people I work, live, or go out with
- ○ I could do with the money
- ○ It smells, makes the house dirty, and clings to clothes
- ○ I don't want to get cancer
- ○ It's anti-social
- ○ I don't like being addicted

_____

_____

_____

_____

'I might get run down by a bus tomorrow' are not actually saying 'the statistics show that I am more likely to get run down by a bus than killed by my smoking.' They probably don't know the statistics, which in fact say the opposite. What they are really saying is 'I don't want to stop, leave me alone.' You will know from your own experience that arguing the statistics is pretty pointless. Just for the record, what are the chances of being killed on the roads of Britain compared with the chances of being killed by cigarettes? The figures overleaf are from the work of the eminent medical scientist Sir Richard Peto, Professor of Medical Statistics and Epidemiology at Oxford University.

Among an average **1000 20-years-olds** in the UK who smoke cigarettes regularly:

about **1** will be murdered
about **6** will die from traffic accidents
about **250** will be killed by smoking in middle age (35–69) alone
(**250** more will die in old age from smoking)

IT WON'T HAPPEN TO ME

It is often said that smokers know that smoking is harmful. This is not really true or at best is only a half-truth. It is true that if you ask smokers if smoking is bad for the health many will say 'yes'. But that is very different from asking them if they think they personally will suffer ill health as a result of their smoking, or if they know exactly how dangerous it is.

Most of us prefer not to think about the future consequences of our unhealthy actions and think, or at least hope, that we will get away with it. Of course it's possible that we will, but it can be a risky strategy and is a rather passive one. Unfortunately with smoking it is particularly risky because the chances of smokers suffering ill health as a result of their smoking are disturbingly high. They are a lot higher than most smokers realize. Even in countries where there has been a lot of education and information about smoking most smokers have little idea just how dangerous smoking is. Do you?

We also tend to underestimate our chances of suffering some particular risks and to overestimate our chances of getting away with them. For example, would you cross a motorway blindfolded?

The risk of dying from different causes calculated over a ten-year period during mid life (earthquake figure from California):

Air disaster	1 in 10,000,000
Earthquake	1 in 60,000
Leukaemia	1 in 1250
Car accident	1 in 600
Motor cycle accident	1 in 50
Twenty cigarettes a day	1 in 25

The figure showing the risk of dying from smoking is lower than the figure mentioned elswhere in this chapter because it is not the risk over your whole lifetime. It is only the risk during a narrow ten-year period in middle age. Even in such a short space of time it is a lot more dangerous to be a smoker than a motorcycle or car driver.

Approximate annual deaths in England from different causes:

Smoking	90,000
Road accidents	4000
Suicide	4000
Liver cirrhosis	3000
Infectious diseases like measles	2000

Imagine you are standing at the edge of a motorway. It is about 3 am and traffic is quiet. An expert who has been doing some research on traffic flow has established that if you walk blindfolded across the motorway now, you only have a one in four chance of being knocked down and killed. Would you do it? I have never yet met anyone who says they would do it, for any reward, even those who might bet on a horse whose odds of winning are 10 to 1 against. Yet the chances of dying prematurely as a result of smoking used to be reckoned at one in four, and are now reckoned at one in two over your whole lifetime, according to research by Sir Richard Peto published in the *British Medical Journal*. Half of you will suffer directly as a result of your smoking. That is an incredibly high chance. Continuing to smoke in the face of those odds is not so much risky as reckless. Of course there are differences between the two events, but the interesting point is the way smokers underestimate their chances of being damaged by smoking and overestimate their chances of getting away with it.

WHY THEY STOPPED

'I gave up because I was pregnant. After the baby I was breastfeeding so I didn't smoke, and after that I thought I'd better be healthy so I'll be around to look after my kids for as long as possible. It wasn't difficult because the motivation was so massive. I wanted a healthy baby.' **Marion, 39**

'One other contributing factor was that I had been to the dentist to get my teeth polished for the wedding and noticed the amount of tar that was taken from between my lower front teeth. I also didn't want my teeth to stain again before the wedding.' **Dylan, 35**

'It got to the point where I was doing a lot more exercise and was a lot more aware of my health, which is why I'd cut down. My grandfather had emphysema which also made me more aware of my health. I finally gave up on the day that he died. I'd never actually decided that I wanted to give up before the time that I actually did. I knew on the day that he died that I'd give up, and I did.' **Vicky, 24**

'Looking back, it was my own strong motivation that did it. My wife had given up the previous year. She'd had hypnosis – well, it worked for her. I scoffed at it but I was interested in what she was trying to do. My daughter was a motivator. She was 12. She'd hassle you.' **Sean, 59**

'I've always wanted to give up smoking because I've never really liked the idea of smoking. But I've always enjoyed smoking. I certainly don't like the idea of polluting my body now, because I'm older and thinking about having children (in the future) and I think it's about being with someone who I actually want to have children with, makes it more real. Toby didn't say till the other day that he doesn't like me smoking because it's harming me, so that wasn't actually put on me.' **Sally, 26**

'I think the other thing is that I tried to give up with Sally, so there was that additional competitive element. A bit of pride in it.' **Toby, 29**

'It's a funny story. I met a guy who I knew 35 years ago when I was 14. We fell in love. He was smoking like crazy so I said "I love you so much, I want to spend my life with you but if we are still smoking like this we will have to help each other with oxygen." He was very skinny and he had a problem breathing. He was very afraid because he never stopped before. I tried many times, up to 12 years ago. We planned everything together. I said to myself "I'm going to buy some nicotine gum." I went to the drugstore but the pharmacist said "You should try the patches." So I bought some and took them home. We read the instructions and we fixed the date. We talked a lot about stopping. He was more afraid than I was. On November 8th we put a patch on and we stopped. Afterwards we talked a lot about it – we didn't smell bad, we could breathe better.' **Odette, 50**

PROBLEMS OR EXCUSES?

Do you find that as soon as you start thinking seriously about stopping, lots of problems suddenly start popping into your mind? If so, you need to ask yourself, are they real problems or are they excuses? If they are real problems, you are going to work out how to deal with them. But what is probably going on is that the part of your brain that is addicted knows what is coming and is afraid. It doesn't want to go through withdrawal. It just wants to continue with its cosy little addiction and is trying to put you off by coming up with all the problems it can possibly think of, in the hope you will abandon your plan to stop smoking. Ignore it. Distinguish between genuine problems and excuses and face the excuses now. How many of these sound familiar?

This isn't the right time

There are bad times to stop, for example when you are under special stress. Common sense tells us that it is not a good time if we have just lost our job, moved house, or the car has been in an accident. That is a problem. But this can also be used as an excuse. The right time to stop is as soon as possible – always assuming, that is, that you want to.

Even if you are dealing with difficult problems in your life, it might still help to stop smoking now. Take Greta, who came to my stop smoking course. She was 40, smoked about 25–30 a day, and was living with her ageing and invalided mother, with whom she seemed to have a combative, rather difficult relationship. It seemed that she could not break away from her mother and felt both very attached to her and very undermined by her. She had very low self-esteem.

At the end of the first session, she wanted to know whether, in view of how difficult her life was, I thought she should try and stop smoking or should leave it until a happier time in her life. I think she wanted me to sympathize with her situation, which I did, and then give her permission not to have to go through with stopping smoking. I did that also, and offered advice on where else she might get help for her problems. She was grateful and was just about to leave when I added that occasionally, people in such an apparently difficult situation found that if they could manage to stop, it helped them in other areas of their life because stopping boosted their self-esteem. I suggested she should think about this and at least consider the idea. She did. She came back the following week, went through the course, and stopped smoking. Although she had not found it easy, she seemed very determined and quietly confident, and she was still not smoking six months later.

It's too late – the damage is probably done

If you stop smoking before you get any serious disease, like cancer, bronchitis or heart disease, you are very likely to remain healthy. This is because the danger from smoking builds up over many years. The sooner you stop, the safer you will be, but it is always worth stopping.

Last time the withdrawal symptoms were too bad

You can learn from earlier attempts to stop, and avoid any obvious mistakes this time. The key to overcoming withdrawal symptoms, including craving, is really wanting to stop. There are also treatments to help with the withdrawal, especially nicotine replacement therapy (NRT), which have been proved to work. For more information on NRT, see **NRT and other aids to stopping**, p. 90.

I may put on weight

The average weight gain when smokers stop is quite small, usually only a few pounds. Be careful with your diet and only eat what you would normally. But it's better to lose any weight gain once you are a non-smoker, and this is what most smokers do. For more information on diet and exercise, see **Stopping**, p. 56.

In Britain alone, over the last 20 years or so, over **10 million people** have stopped smoking.

This is over **1000 people every day.** It can be done.

I haven't got any willpower

Don't underestimate your willpower. Rollo May, an American psychologist, called willpower the most under-used resource of the twentieth century. He believed that if people worked harder to find out what they really wanted, and then focused on getting it, there would be no limit to what they could achieve. The mistake people

BRIDGET · 50

'I mean I always felt I must give up smoking. My mother had died of lung cancer and so every time I smoked I felt I was getting closer to the grave. But I was too addicted to be able to do it. Until one New Year's Eve we were having a party at home and my husband and another chap said that they were going to give up smoking and I thought "I'm going to give it up too". They said women had no willpower and that made me do it. So from then on I have never smoked. And my husband gave up at the same time. He couldn't keep it up!'

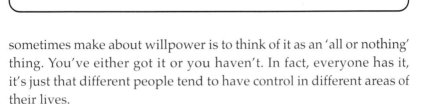

> 'The main thing that kept me going was the thought "I can prove it to myself and everyone else." It was like an endurance test. Although everyone supported me I did feel like they were waiting for me to fail.'

VICKY · 24

sometimes make about willpower is to think of it as an 'all or nothing' thing. You've either got it or you haven't. In fact, everyone has it, it's just that different people tend to have control in different areas of their lives.

For example, if I eat one piece of chocolate I find it extremely difficult not to eat another, and another. So when I go on a diet I have to give up chocolate completely. I really don't have much self-control with chocolate, but most of the time it doesn't particularly bother me. In other areas of my life I can be disciplined if I need to be. If I need to work morning, afternoon and evening for a while – say a month – to get a job done, I can do it. I don't like it but I can do it if there is a strong enough reason. At school I did very badly in my mock A levels. My teacher looked me in the eye and said 'Raw, if you're going to do well in the exam there's going to have to be a minor miracle by the summer.' I was so angry I thought 'I'll ... well show you'. And I did. By challenging me (or goading me) he motivated me and engaged – or rather made me engage – my willpower.

Build up your willpower. Find some part of your life where you are very determined, perhaps something you like doing, or something which is a priority for you. Something you give up other things for, and go out of your way to make sure it doesn't get interrupted. That's willpower. Organizing your life around something. You've got it. You just have to learn to apply it to something new: stopping smoking.

ARE YOU READY?

You have thought about your reasons for stopping smoking, admitted to the things you may miss about it, and are now thinking about the next steps. You need to ask yourself 'Am I going to stop?' and 'Am I ready?' If this feels a bit scary, I am going to repeat myself. Don't go on unless you are sure you want to. If you want to stop but you are afraid, because you think it will be difficult, then I have some good news. Firstly, the most important ingredient of success is your desire to stop. Secondly, there is help around: friends and family, help to cope with the withdrawal particularly in the form of nicotine replacement therapy (NRT) and other treatments, and in the rest of this book.

There are only two things to hold you back now. One is that you don't really want to stop. The other is that you are afraid to stop. Reading the rest of this book will help you deal with the fear and take you in stages through the process of stopping.

DON'T GIVE UP

Millions of smokers have been down this road before you, so you are in really good company. If at any stage you feel you can't go on, for whatever reason, don't feel guilty and don't punish yourself. Take a break then go back to the appropriate stage in the book and start again. This book is not about pain and suffering. It is about planning carefully and going at your own speed. It's about helping you achieve what you want to achieve. It's about helping you conquer your addiction and enjoy a healthier, fuller life. It may interest you to know that most smokers say they found it easier to stop smoking than they thought they would. This is the time to remember that what you are about to do is not a negative thing. You are not going to deprive yourself of something (except an addictive drug). You are going to give yourself a better life.

ARE YOU READY TO STOP?

Ask yourself these questions...

Are you sure you want to stop?	Yes	No
Are you sure of your reasons?	Yes	No
Are you ready to start making a plan?	Yes	No

As Deirdre put it after she stopped: 'Now I look at my money and my health and on balance I prefer to be a non-smoker. I still want to smoke but I want to be a non-smoker even more. I really believe you can only succeed if you feel you have gained something. It's not just a negative thing.'

If you answer 'no' to any of the questions above, you need to go back over this chapter. If you answer yes to all three, you are ready to continue.

You might want to go out and buy a notebook at this point, in case you don't want to carry this book around with you all the time. However, at the end of the book we've left a few blank pages which you can use for notes. You will find it useful to have somewhere to jot down thoughts on stopping, and particularly to have a record to hand of your reasons for stopping and your plan.

STAGE 1

STAGE 2

STAGE 3

STAGE 4

THINKING ABOUT
STOPPING

PREPARING TO
STOP

1000

people a day
STOP
smoking

STOPPING

STAYING
STOPPED

There are three important steps in preparing to stop:
1. Know what you are up against.
2. Remember why you are doing this.
3. Make an action plan.

But first, why prepare at all? Why bother? Why not just do it? Because planning ahead, anticipating difficulties and working out how you are going to deal with them is the key to success. Most people will succeed better at any large or complex task by good planning. And the better prepared you are, the easier it will be.

Supposing you decided that you wanted to run a marathon. Marathons have been run by people in their 80s, but whatever your age you could never just go out and run one. You would need to train over quite a long period before you'd be in good enough shape to run 26 miles. The same applies to stopping smoking.

Ian planned his stop smoking programme very carefully, especially the timing, so that he would have been without cigarettes for a long time already when his most stressful work period arrived. He also reorganized other aspects of his life to take the pressure off him. In other words, while he was stopping, he cleared other things out of the way to make stopping smoking a priority – and it worked.

'I sat down and thought I won't do it now because I'm getting into school term, so I decided that I would rearrange some other aspects of my life too and shed some responsibilities outside school. I put it together as a package. I decided to give up at the start of the spring term and have ten weeks with the nicotine patches. This would take me to the Easter hols which would be a relaxing time and then the summer term would not be quite as stressful. Then I would get through to the summer hols so that when I got to September and pressure I would have given up for eight months. The patches broke the nicotine addiction but I had to break the habit... At the beginning, I used to bore my mates silly by saying "It's the sixth day etc" but then they told me to shut up. I stopped thinking about it after about three months. The first couple of days I went without any patches I felt ever so proud because I got through them. Basically, I stopped because I had a plan, I was in control. I didn't just say I'm going to stop and then just do it and probably fail. I didn't want to fail, I wanted to succeed. That's why I planned it for three or four months with one or two other bits and pieces of change in lifestyle.' **Ian, 51**

KNOW WHAT YOU
ARE UP AGAINST

Smoking is an extremely strong habit and it is also a drug addiction. Let's take the habit first.

Repetitive brain injury

One of the great psychologists of the mid-twentieth century, Clark Hull, described what a habit is in terms of what happens to the nerve pathways in the brain. A particular behaviour (like smoking) uses a particular set of nerves along a particular route. The more the behaviour is repeated, the more that set of nerves along that particular route is used; the more they are used, the smoother the route becomes. Eventually a pathway is formed by constant use. This means that the electrical nerve impulses pass along this route because connections have formed – it becomes the easiest way to go. Hull made an almost exact comparison with a pathway being worn in a field or a forest by constant use, so that when you come to walk through the forest you naturally take the easiest route – the one already worn.

The same thing applies to smoking. How many times do you perform the simple act of bringing the cigarette to your mouth and inhaling the smoke? Just think about it. If you take an average of 10 puffs a cigarette and smoke 20 cigarettes a day, that's 200 puffs a day, 1400 a week, 6000 a month, 72,000 a year. That adds up to around 1 to 2 million puffs from the time you started to the time you realize you'd better stop in middle age. That is a lot of repetitions, a strongly worn nerve pathway. Enough to make a habit very well established and very difficult to shift for many smokers.

TOBY · 29

'I did actually try the chewing gum before, on a previous attempt. When I was getting nicotine from something else, it made me realize how much I was actually chasing the nicotine when I was actually smoking, whereas I'd always thought I just liked smoking, just for the taste and the pleasure of smoking. I never really clicked that I was a nicotine junky.'

Effects of the drug

Scientists are now calling cigarettes drug delivery devices. Over the last few decades the tobacco industry has refined and developed the cigarette into an incredibly efficient device for delivering doses of nicotine to your brain quickly and with maximum chemical effect. Even as I write, we are learning more and more about the tobacco industry's research and development from confidential documents released as a result of court cases. The modern cigarette is a cleverly designed and engineered device for delivering nicotine to the brain in doses which will have a maximum effect physiologically.

It only takes seven seconds for the nicotine in just one puff to cross from the lungs into the blood system and on to the brain. That is twice as fast as if you injected the drug into your arm. The only way you could get the nicotine into the brain more quickly would be to inject it direct into the artery in your neck (which could kill you). And just to make the whole process run more smoothly, many additives and flavouring agents are added to the tobacco to make it more 'palatable' or easy to inhale. You may wonder why you, as a consumer of this product, are not allowed to know what its ingredients are and why such a dangerous product has such minimal and uninformative labelling. If you are interested in some of the ingredients of tobacco smoke (there are more than 4000), see **More facts about smoking,**

p. 101. It is not pretty reading. It includes chemicals like ammonia, arsenic, benzene, carbon monoxide, chromium, formaldehyde, cyanide, lead, phenol, urethane and many, many others.

A deadly combination

What makes smoking so addictive is the combination of the simplicity of the behaviour needed to smoke and the extremely quick and powerful effect of the drug on the brain. Some people say 'If it's so addictive how come so many smokers stop?' But if it's not addictive how come so many smokers continue smoking until it kills them? Calling something an addiction doesn't mean it is impossible to stop, it just means it is difficult. But an awful lot of smokers do not manage to stop. Just in Britain alone there are still more than 10 million smokers and throughout the world thousands of millions. Richard Peto, Professor of Medical Statistics and Epidemiology at Oxford University, estimates that there have been 100 million deaths caused by smoking in the twentieth century. If current trends continue, particularly in the developing world, he estimates that this will rise to 900 million deaths in the twenty-first century. Not a very impressive example of progress, is it?

REMEMBER WHY YOU ARE DOING THIS

There may be times over the next few months when you are tempted to give up giving up and need to remember your reasons. This is when you will need to refer to what you wrote in this book or in a notebook (or both). You may also find it useful to refresh your memory on some of the facts about smoking (see **More facts about smoking**, p. 101) or to look again at the stories in this book of smokers who gave up. Try to find a few minutes at the beginning and end of each day if possible, to remember your reasons and go over your plan.

JAMES · 48

'I was smoking 20 a day throughout my 20s and first wanted to stop when I was about 25. I think I tried to make a New Year's resolution every year, but it never lasted too long. I got increasingly worried about my health, nothing dramatic, but just that I got a bit short of breath. I suddenly decided when I got into my 30s that I wanted to be healthy for the rest of my life. I remember thinking this on my 30th birthday. I read somewhere that every day you have to think about reasons for stopping, so I wrote down three reasons on a card and looked at it several times a day. I know that saving money was one of the reasons, but I can't remember the others. I remember that I used to take out my girlfriend (my future wife) for a meal once a week, using the money I would have spent on cigarettes. I haven't smoked from that day to this – 18 years. One of the things that probably helped me was the fact that my girlfriend hated cigarette smoke and I don't think she'd have married me if I hadn't given up. I remember I used to think about smoking quite a lot afterwards, probably for about a year, but only at certain times, especially when I was tired and finding it difficult to concentrate on my work.'

GRAHAM · 36

'This time, I just sort of decided. I was lighting up a fag and I wasn't really enjoying it. Also I went to see the doctor and he told me that I had high blood pressure, but by then I'd already really made my mind up. I had a few fags left, I think I threw them away before I went to bed on the Sunday night. It was Monday 14th May 1997. I know the date because it's my mother's birthday. I chose the Monday to stop because I'd be in work and I'd be able to keep busy. The craving would be worse at home. I didn't use any nicotine replacement, but I did have my own aid to stopping. I Tippexed a pencil leaving just the end brown so it looked like a fag. I used this for about 3–4 weeks. I'm a really fidgety person and always need something to do with my hands. That's why I had my pencil idea.'

DYLAN · 35

'I decided to give up smoking during the most stressful time of my life, two weeks before getting married and at one of the busiest times I've ever had at work. I was working ahead of time because I was taking three weeks off work for a honeymoon. My theory was that if giving up smoking makes you stressed then the best time to give up is when your stress is at its highest – you have something else to blame for the stress.

MAKE AN
ACTION PLAN

A good plan has a timetable, anticipates problems, includes support and plans rewards. We are going to go through these one by one. Remember though, that this is your plan. When it is complete, make sure you are happy with it. If you are, it will work.

Choose a day

Will you be more relaxed during the week or at the weekend? Or does it make no difference? Will it be better for you to stop when things are quiet (if they ever are) or when they are busy? If it helps, keep a record of your smoking for a few days so that you can see when you smoke and what you were doing when you lit up. This will help you decide what day to stop and will help you plan how to deal with difficult situations and times. If you smoke more than 30 a day, or want to record your smoking for a week or more, use a notebook. Choose the best day but not too far ahead. Give yourself time to complete your preparation but not time to put it off.

DEIRDRE · 24

'I was keeping a calendar this year of the times I smoked and the times I didn't. I looked at it one day and I thought "this is stupid." I also added up the money. Then finally one day in June I just thought "this is ridiculous" and I thought, no, that's it.'

ONE-DAY SMOKING CHART

	TIME	WHAT WERE YOU DOING?
1		
2		
3		
4		
5		
6		
7		
8		
9		
10		
11		
12		
13		
14		
15		
16		
17		
18		
19		
20		
21		
22		
23		
24		
25		
26		
27		
28		
29		
30		

Anticipate problems

What are going to be the key challenges for you on the first day and over the first week? Use the checklist below to think about what they may be and how you will deal with them.

PROBLEM PREDICTOR

On the first day:

The biggest problem will be ...

_____

_____

The solution is ...

_____

_____

During the first week:

The biggest problem will be ...

_____

_____

The solution is ...

_____

_____

Other problems during the first week ...

_____

_____

Solutions ...

_____

_____

_____

SEAN · 59

'I had meant to stop on 1 January 1988 but I decided to leave it for a bit. I was at a New Year party and I told the people I was giving up at the end of January. They all laughed. The people at the party were mostly work colleagues. I wanted to stop badly – the family, my doctor, health reasons, you know. I'd had two fainting fits – I thought it was the smoking. So that February I put a notice up in the staff room to say I was stopping smoking and I went round telling everybody. My wife was really supportive while I was giving up.'

Dealing with problems

Among the common problems smokers describe are:
- family (including a partner), friends or colleagues who smoke
- when smoking is part of a routine (when the phone goes, with coffee, after a meal, with alcohol)
- stressful situations like difficult meetings or arguments

Family, friends and colleagues who smoke

What about smokers who offer you cigarettes because they don't know you are stopping? Do you tell people you are stopping or keep quiet about it? Some people keep quiet about the fact they are stopping, so they don't put themselves under pressure from other people's expectations. Sean, on the other hand, made sure his friends and colleagues knew that he was stopping.

What do you do about those smokers who know you are stopping but continue to offer you cigarettes? It could be that they are jealous. You're doing what they want to do. Try to avoid them. If that fails, or if they are really persistent, you could always try what a friend of mine did, very successfully he said. He took the cigarette he was offered and slowly broke it up in front of his tormentor, who never bothered him again. Incidentally my friend also took up knitting so that he had something to do with his hands!

If your partner smokes, the obvious answer is to discuss it with them and if they don't want to stop themselves, at least ask them to be considerate and not make life more difficult for you. Vicky's partner wasn't entirely helpful: 'He lit up a cigarette in front of me, I was so ****** off. I got really angry. Generally though, he was quite supportive, except for smoking in front of me, he did want me to give up.' But all you can do really is try to make them see how important this is for you, and negotiate. Failing that do what Vicky did and make it motivate you, 'but the main thing that kept me going was the thought "I can prove it to myself and everyone else."'

Spencer found that his girlfriend's smoking put him off: 'I live with my girlfriend and she smokes. In fact her whole family do, so I am quite exposed. However, the more they tend to smoke the more it puts me off. In fact if there are four of them smoking in the same room it often makes me want to pop out for some fresh air and I think "God, is that what I did? Why did I do it?" and sometimes it makes me want to puke.'

PARTNERS WHO SMOKE

Please at least consider stopping with your partner, but if you don't want to do that, you can still help a lot by being considerate and supportive. Offer as much help and support as you can, reinforce their determination to stop and get involved in helping them make an action plan. Please don't offer them cigarettes, or leave your cigarettes lying around, or smoke near him or her. The least you owe your partner is to respect their choice.

When smoking is part of a routine

Smoking is strongly linked to certain times, places and situations: like the first cigarette of the day, the cigarette with tea or coffee, when the phone rings. The situations will vary but the principle of how you deal with them is the same. You should try to break the link between the situation and smoking by changing your routines. For example, drink orange or something else instead of coffee for a while. The same applies to established patterns of behaviour. If you would find it impossible to spend an evening in a pub or a bar with friends without smoking, then you may have to consider cutting out these evenings temporarily. If you are using NRT as part of your stop smoking plan use some before going into that situation. It won't completely take away the temptation, but it will boost your nicotine level a bit and take the edge off the craving enough to make it easier to cope. Sally (see p. 44) stopped smoking when her whole life changed in a major way. Although you may not be able to plan something so major just to stop smoking, if there is some big change on the way, could it be the time to stop? Any change of routine can help break old habits.

Be aware that smoking with a meal can induce a craving for a cigarette. When you eat, blood is diverted to the stomach and as the food is digested, the levels of any drug in the blood (not just nicotine) will fall. You may not be conscious of this but your brain and body will be and will crave more nicotine.

IAN · 51

'I would leave home at six to get to the bus stop at five past so I had time to have a cigarette before the bus came. I now leave at five past six … so I don't have to stand at the bus stop.'

SALLY · 26

'When I quit in January I had recently started working full time at the hospital and had started a new routine during the day, which is probably important. I was starting a new job, nobody knew I smoked, there was no smoking room, no smoking breaks. It was a new job and it was very different. It was easier to be a non-smoker because nobody had ever known me as a smoker. Another thing that helped encourage me not to smoke, was that around that time, I didn't have a method of contraception sorted out and therefore kept thinking I was pregnant, and if I was then I didn't want to damage the child.'

BRIDGET · 50

'It was torture for the first three weeks. I couldn't sit down and have a cup of coffee because I associated coffee and a cigarette. I couldn't associate with any of my friends who smoked because the first time I did, when a friend came round for a chat, I began almost to hallucinate – I could see smoke coming out of every orifice in her body. She chain-smoked. I didn't hear a word she said … I was hallucinating. But I think I was sort of trying to desensitize myself by thinking: "Look what she's doing to her body," trying to feel the danger in front of me. And then I just stopped seeing people, just told them till I was over it I would isolate myself from smoking – which I did. It was at least a month before I could see them.'

Stressful situations

Many smokers reach for a cigarette when they feel stressed. But in fact, there is very little scientific evidence that smoking helps people cope with stress. Smokers as a whole tend to be more stressed than non-smokers not less, and the feeling that smoking helps you cope with stress is more to do with addiction and withdrawal from nicotine.

Smokers get used to smoking in such a way that they maintain a steady blood nicotine level, by the number of cigarettes, the time between each one, the number of puffs from each, how deeply each puff is inhaled. A cigarette allows very precise control over the nicotine dose. According to a former research director of a tobacco company: 'People smoke for nicotine. So you can look upon each cigarette as an injection of nicotine. You can get an immediate feeling of well-being by injecting yourself through your lungs with the smoke. It happens in three to eight seconds – so fast, compared to other drugs, that you feel it's instantaneous.'

This means that when you have got over the withdrawal, you will be able to cope with stress as well as you did when you were still smoking. In fact, the evidence suggests you may cope better. But while you are stopping you are in withdrawal. Nicotine replacement therapy can help with this (see **NRT and other aids to stopping**, p. 90). Learning ways of coping with stress will also help. Here are some suggestions:

Change your thinking

Get into the habit of counteracting negative thoughts by identifying what thought is making you feel stressed or depressed, and thinking of another thought that will counteract the negative thought. For example:

NEGATIVE THOUGHT If I don't have a fag, I won't be able to face people.
COPING THOUGHT It will be difficult but I've done it before.
NEGATIVE THOUGHT I'm bound to give an awful presentation this morning, I haven't done enough preparation.
COPING THOUGHT It doesn't matter if I speak for less than half an hour. I'll go over the main points on my way to work.

Simple steps to relieve tension

Laughter really is the best medicine. Laughing is your body's natural stress release. Make time for laughter. Rent your favourite comedy video. Tape a television show that makes you laugh and keep it handy for stress emergencies. Go to the library and borrow a book by an author who can make you laugh. Read the daily comics in the newspaper. Phone someone who makes you laugh.

Walk away from the stress. On your coffee break, lunch hour or when you're at home, try going for a stress-relieving and energizing walk instead of sitting down for another cup of stress-inducing caffeine. It's easier to walk off your urges to smoke than wash them away with a drink. If you don't like walking by yourself, find someone to join you (or take the dog).

Sit back, breathe deeply and relax. When you feel anxious your breathing tends to become quick and shallow. This is called hyper-ventilation and will make you feel more stressed and anxious. Try breathing deeply and slowly and feel the tension flow out of your body every time you breathe out (see opposite).

Reduce stress levels

Set goals at achievable levels. Failing to achieve goals adds to your stress levels. Try to reward yourself as you reach each goal.

Become more active. Get fit, feel great. Exercise is a very effective way of releasing tension and improving mood. Regular exercise has been shown to increase a chemical called serotonin in the brain. This is one of the chemicals that helps us to feel less depressed.

Increase social interaction. People and pets can be an important source of comfort. Spend more time with them.

Set aside time to relax. Physical relaxation techniques like meditation and yoga are useful in preventing stress and lowering your physical signs of stress.

Learn how to relax

You can improve your relaxation by consciously controlling your breathing. Try these exercises.

Exhalation breathing

- Lie on your back with your arms at your sides.
- As you begin to inhale (breathe in), raise your arms towards the ceiling (elbows bent). Move your arms all the way up and over your head to the floor as you inhale.
- Reverse the order: exhale (breathe out) slowly and smoothly as you return your arms to your sides.
- After you have done this several times, slowly inhale and exhale without moving your arms. You can do this exercise for ten minutes or longer – it's up to you. It is simple yet can slow you down quite effectively.

Deep breathing

You can do this anytime, anywhere. Deep breathing provides extra oxygen to the blood and causes the body to release endorphins, which are naturally occurring hormones that re-energize and promote relaxation. Do this exercise for three to five minutes whenever you feel tense.

- Slowly inhale through your nose, expanding your abdomen before allowing air to fill your lungs.
- Reverse the process as you exhale.

Muscular relaxation

This technique helps relax tense muscles and has a deep relaxing effect on the mind. At first, it may take about 20 minutes, but with practice, you'll be able to do it in about five minutes.

- Sit or lie down on your back in a comfortable, quiet room. Close your eyes.
- Clench your fists tight, hold for five seconds, then relax your hands. Do this three times. Pay attention to the different sensations of tension and relaxation.

- Repeat with the muscles in your arms, shoulders, chest, abdomen, back, hips, thighs, lower legs and feet.

Stretching exercises
If done correctly, stretching can promote relaxation and reduce stress. Never bounce when you stretch – you could injure your muscles. Do each of these exercises for five or ten minutes.

For any muscles:
- Decide which muscles to stretch.
- As you stretch, think about one area that's being stretched. Imagine the tension leaving as you gently take this area to its comfortable limit.
- Exhale into the stretch; inhale on the release. Breathe deeply and slowly – do not hold your breath.
- Close your eyes for better awareness of your body's responses.

For stiff muscles:
- Sit up straight and inhale.
- Exhale as you let your head move down to your chest. You'll feel a gentle stretch on the back of your neck and your shoulders.
- Roll your right ear toward your right shoulder while inhaling. Drop your chin to your chest again while exhaling. Repeat to the left.
- Drop your arms to your sides and push both shoulders forward. Slowly raise them towards your ears and circle them back and downward to the starting point. After two or three rotations, change directions.

Get support

You don't have to stop smoking on your own. If you need help and support (which is almost like saying if you are human), get it. Does this sound ridiculously obvious? It is amazing how hard we sometimes are on ourselves and how we can completely forget to do simple, obvious things to make our lives easier, like getting help. We don't want to bother people, we think we don't deserve help, or we think it's our responsibility and no-one else's! What a sad world we live in when we feel we can't pick up the phone or call round to a friend and say 'Can I have a chat?' It's as if we feel we don't deserve to be happy or successful. So if you think you will benefit from a bit of sympathetic support, go and find it. Even better, find another smoker who wants to stop and keep in touch over the phone, or meet occasionally if possible. Write their number in a notebook. Choose someone you can ring if you need encouragement. Someone you would be happy to hear from if they need support. Be selfish about this. It will only be for a few weeks or months at the most and you deserve it!

You may also be able to get useful support or advice from your doctor, nurse, pharmacists, or even a stop smoking treatment course. Think of this in a very practical way. As you make your plan, put into it all the things you are going to need, then take as long as necessary to arrange these things, including help if you need it.

Plan rewards

Plan a reward for the end of day one and the end of week one. You just need to be careful that it is not something that will clash with your ultimate goal of stopping smoking. You may need a bit of creative thinking here and it could be helpful to discuss this with a partner, friend or fellow stopper. The problem with the obvious rewards, some nice food or drink, is that the first might lead to weight gain, which could undermine your stop attempt, and the second could just undermine your attempt because of its effect on motivation. I'm not saying don't reward yourself at the end of the first day or week with a nice meal or drink. I am just saying be careful and be sensible.

Even in one week, in countries where cigarettes are not as expensive as they are in northern Europe, you will have saved enough money to go to the cinema. And an average 20 a day smoker in Britain will have saved enough in one week to go to the cinema and have a meal (although probably without alcohol). Ask yourself at the end of each day 'Have I been kind to myself today?' and if you have not, do something about it.

COMMONLY ASKED
QUESTIONS

Should I cut down gradually first?

If you find yourself tempted to try to cut down slowly, first ask yourself
if you've ever tried it before, or if you know anyone else who tried it?
If so, what happened? It can be a useful step towards stopping, but it
can also make things even more difficult. All you need to ask yourself
is 'Do I want to cut down because I think it will work, or is it because
I am afraid to stop?' If it is because you are afraid to stop it won't work,
obviously, because then it's not about stopping, it's about the opposite:
putting off stopping. Some smokers opt for gradual reduction because
they are afraid to stop, and one of its disadvantages is that you are
constantly thinking about cigarettes, working out when you can have
the next one. That can make the withdrawal symptoms much worse.

Quite a lot of the questions asked by smokers who are thinking
about stopping reveal the fact that they are not yet ready to stop. They
ask because they are really hoping the answer will allow them to put
off the day they actually stop smoking. Like the next question.

Can I just switch to low tar cigarettes?

The problem with low tar cigarettes is they usually contain less
nicotine as well as tar. This means that smokers inhale more smoke
to get the same amount of nicotine. In fact, doctors are now detecting
an increase in a once rare form of lung cancer deep in the lung.
'Normal' lung cancer suffered by smokers is in the bronchial tubes or
close to the top of the lung, in other words where the tobacco smoke
is deposited when you breathe it in. It looks as if smokers inhaling
much more deeply on low tar cigarettes, to get the fix of nicotine, have
tar being deposited much deeper in the lung, causing this new type
of lung cancer.

Evidence that has emerged recently from the tobacco industry,
particularly from a retired research director of one tobacco company,

shows that the industry saw low tar cigarettes not as in any way less dangerous than ordinary cigarettes, but as a marketing strategy. They realized that if smokers thought low tar cigarettes were less dangerous they might switch to them instead of stopping smoking altogether. And that is what has probably happened to thousands, if not millions of smokers. The result of this pretty cynical tobacco industry plan is almost certainly more deaths than would have happened if smokers had just stopped.

Should I keep some cigarettes, just in case?

Just in case what? You want to smoke? I have actually met smokers in my groups who did this. Somehow they didn't feel quite so panicky if they knew they could have one just in case, and I admit that it worked for some of them. Some smokers say that losing cigarettes can feel a little like bereavement and that the sense of loss can be alleviated sometimes by having some connection with or reminder of the lost object, in this case cigarettes. However, I don't think it's a good idea for most smokers. I'm certain that most smokers who find themselves asking the question are hoping for a comforting answer that will let them off the hook. This question is similar to the first two and you have probably already ruled all three out of your plan by now. On simple logical grounds the answer has got to be no. When I decide to lose weight or eat less fatty food, I don't stock my fridge and cupboards up with burgers, chocolate and beer. I empty the house of these things so that when I feel the craving, and it feels like a craving sometimes, I can't give in.

What are withdrawal symptoms and how long will they last?

I have explained that when you stop smoking you are withdrawing from the drug nicotine and from a deeply ingrained habit. It takes time for the drug to be cleared from the body and for the habit to weaken. During this time you may suffer withdrawal from both. In fact, nicotine is not the only drug from which you will be withdrawing. There are so many chemicals in tobacco smoke that we still don't know exactly what effect they all have on the body. The nicotine and carbon monoxide are normally gone within days but it is possible that some of the other chemicals take much longer than this.

The most commonly experienced withdrawal symptoms are hunger, sleep disturbance, depression, lightheadedness, irritability, anxiety, restlessness, poor concentration and craving. Smokers with higher nicotine levels do get worse withdrawal symptoms, although nicotine replacement therapy (NRT) and exercise actually reduce their intensity. Stress and boredom also seem to make withdrawal worse. In the end, however, what causes the withdrawal is less important than how you cope with it.

NRT will help (but will not provide a total or totally satisfying alternative). Other treatment and support will help some smokers. Exercise can help as well. But perhaps most important of all, remaining single-minded and absolutely focused will provide the best guarantee of success. I have seen so many smokers over the years whose withdrawal symptoms got worse as soon as they started questioning whether it was worth stopping. It's a positive feedback circuit. Doubts creep in so the withdrawal gets worse. The withdrawal gets worse so the doubts get worse. That is why you should keep this book or your notebook with your reasons for stopping close by. If you ever feel your resolve weakening, read it, then if necessary talk to a friend (or doctor or nurse or pharmacist or anyone).

The good news is that if you are determined and don't give in, the worst will be over in about a month, possibly less. Occasionally withdrawal symptoms last longer, but the most important milestones appear to be one and three months. The research also shows that the longer you succeed the better your chances become of permanent success.

Ian found that the worst was over in three months (from January to Easter). Deirdre knew she had succeeded when she survived a family wedding 10 weeks after stopping. Sean said 'It was a long time, three or four months before I stopped thinking about smoking.' Vicky experienced something similar: 'Three months was a big turning point for me. I suddenly realized that I was going two or three days without thinking about it. The first two weeks were physically quite difficult, but the first two months were very difficult psychologically. After about a year I could go a whole week without thinking about smoking and now I can go at least a month.'

NRT – DO I NEED IT?

To find out if NRT will help you, fill in this chart.

How long is it before you light up your first cigarette after waking up?

0–5 mins

6–30 mins

more than 30 mins

How many cigarettes do you smoke every day?

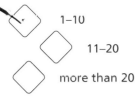

1–10

11–20

more than 20

Do you miss cigarettes if you have to go without them for a while (say, at the cinema or on a bus)?

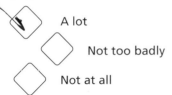

A lot

Not too badly

Not at all

How did you do?

If you light up within five minutes of waking, smoke more than 20 a day and miss cigarettes even for short periods (like during a film), you are very addicted and should try NRT.

If you scored all the middle categories you are quite strongly addicted. NRT is a good choice for you as well.

If you smoke less than 10 a day and don't light up within 30 minutes of waking, or do not miss cigarettes for shortish periods, you are probably not very dependent and may not need NRT. But some light smokers still find it helpful.

However, this is only a very rough guide and there is no strict scientific evidence to say that you will or will not need NRT as part of your programme. If you think you may need it, the best approach is to try it and see if it helps. Make sure you know how to use it. There are more details about NRT in **NRT and other aids to stopping**, p. 90.

READY TO GO

You have decided you want to stop smoking and completed your preparation. Your final task before stopping is to review your plan and make sure everything – or everything under your control anyway – is in place. Go through the checklist opposite and when you are happy with your plan, set your stopping day. Expect the unexpected, and go for it!

The day before, get everything ready, review your plan and get rid of any remaining tobacco. One of the most common withdrawal symptoms is irritability, so try as hard as you can to keep your sense of humour over the next week or so. It will help you a lot.

STOPPING CHECKLIST

 Have I chosen a good day to stop?

 Have I planned how I am going to deal with difficult situations?

 Have I decided if I am going to go public or not?

 If not, am I going to tell anyone at all?

 Friends?

 Partner?

 Family?

 Colleagues?

 Health professionals?

 Am I asking someone specific for support?

 Will I be using NRT or any other treatments?

 Have I decided to get rid of all tobacco?

Have I planned the changes to routines which I'll need?

Have I planned rewards?

THINKING ABOUT
STOPPING

PREPARING TO
STOP

STOPPING

Food tastes better when you **DON'T SMOKE**

STAYING
STOPPED

Make time at the beginning of the first day to go through your plan. Remind yourself again why you are stopping, because, in the end, this is what is going to get you through the first few months.

Whether you have decided to make it a big day, or to treat it as a normal day, don't forget the basic principles and especially don't forget that this is a choice you have made because you want a better life.

Stick to your plan. Keep thinking ahead and anticipating problems. Try not to let anything take you by surprise. Remember how you are going to deal with difficult situations. Be sensible about alcohol (or even take a break from it) and about spending social time with friends who smoke or in smoky places.

However, remember that this is *your* plan and that it has got to work for you. If you follow the principles laid out in this book, your plan will be based on sound scientific principles and good common sense, and it will work. So don't worry if avoiding smoking friends or alcohol

ALISON · 34

'Something that has really struck me about giving up, is how everyone is different. I thought that when I went to the group there would be a way of doing it and it would be the same for everyone. But everyone's different and everyone found it difficult trying to give up. I've got a friend who went to the group as well. She gave up, too, for six months but then she started again. Later on, she went for hypnotherapy, which worked for her and she hasn't smoked since. You have to find the way that's right for you.'

TOP STOP TIPS

- If you need to put something in your mouth try (sugar-free) chewing gum, or something healthy and non-fattening like a carrot.

- If you need to do something with your hands find something to fiddle with – a pencil, coin, worry beads, anything.

- Don't forget the habit-breaking principle – for example you could try drinking orange juice instead of coffee for a while.

- Save your cigarette money – an average smoker in Britain would be able to afford a return ticket to New York after just three months off cigarettes.

- If saving money motivates you and you want to make sure you see these savings you could set up a special savings account, and even make a standing order to it.

- If you want something to remind you what you are leaving behind, clean out an old jam jar and fill it with cigarette butts (yours or someone else's).

for a few weeks sounds a bit hard, or is simply not possible because of the kind of life or job that you have. It is a sensible idea which will work for a lot of smokers while they stop, but some of you will manage in other ways, as Odette did: 'This time I didn't quit the coffee and the wine. I said to myself, "This is the reality, this I can take." People should do that instead of giving up everything at the same time. I think you have to maintain everything in your life the same when you give up smoking.'

At the end of the first day

Give yourself time to reflect on how the day went and don't forget to be kind to yourself. Reward yourself for getting through the first day, even if it is only something small like having a few minutes of peace and quiet on your own.

THE FIRST WEEK

It is particularly during the first few weeks that your careful preparation will pay off. If you feel a hint of rebellion from your old smoking self, review your reasons for stopping and, if necessary, read Stages 1 and 2 again. Start each day by reflecting briefly on how yesterday went, reviewing your plan, and re-dedicating yourself to it.

Make sure you have arranged all the support you need and deserve. Remember to take some time out to relax. Do be kind to yourself. Congratulate yourself and give yourself rewards for stopping smoking. What reward have you planned for the end of day two? What reward have you planned for the end of week one?

When you get the urge to smoke

If this happens, do something that will distract you. Review your reasons, check the money you are saving, cuddle the cat, pat the dog, walk round the block, walk the dog round the block, just don't allow a debate to start in your head about whether you really want to stop. You have already had this debate and reached a conclusion. Recognize such an urge for what it is – a trick your old smoking self is trying to pull on you. You owe it to yourself to ignore such trickery. The more you stick to your original resolution and ignore such wavering, the weaker the wavering will get and the stronger your resolve. Your willpower will grow.

'I had a very short fuse and I was very easily upset. Probably for the first month. It was very, very difficult. I left home I don't know how many times. I just kept barging out.' **Bridget, 50**

DOREEN · 39

'When I got so edgy or irritable that I knew I would explode if I stayed in the house, I would take the dog for a walk. It got so I was going out about ten times a day taking the dog for a walk. The dog must have got absolutely knackered and after a month I reckon his legs were at least an inch shorter.'

DOs AND DON'Ts

Do think positive There will be times when you feel tired and are tempted to give up. Remind yourself why you are stopping. Plan rewards for yourself. Above all be positive; don't waver. Hold your nerve and the difficulties will become easier to overcome.

Do take care Complacency and carelessness could undo you. Don't allow yourself to be tempted. Don't get into difficult situations. Use your common sense.

Don't play games For example 'I'll just have one to prove I've kicked it.' The occasional cigarette will probably trigger craving. Recognize these games for what they are – your addiction fighting back – and stamp on them.

Don't listen to smokers who try to persuade you that 'one cigarette won't hurt.' They are probably jealous.

DURING THE FIRST WEEK

The best thing about the week was ...

_____

_____

The biggest problem was ...

_____

_____

How well did I cope?

_____

_____

How am I going to cope with it over the next few weeks?

_____

_____

Other problems during the first week were ...

_____

_____

Do I need any new ways of coping?

_____

_____

If so, what are they?

_____

_____

My reward for getting through the first week is ...

_____

_____

At the end of the first week

Give yourself 10 to 15 minutes to sit down with the checklist opposite and review the week's progress. What was the best thing about the week? Was it expected or unexpected? What other good things happened during the week? Were there any problems that you did not anticipate? If so, spend time working out how to deal with them and remember to get help or find someone to talk to if you need to.

THE FIRST FEW WEEKS

Remember how many smokers have been down this same road before you:

Sean got through the first few weeks because of his motivation and willpower. When he was asked if there were there any difficult moments he said: 'Yes, after meals, because I was used to smoking then. When I was driving.' How did he get through them? 'Pure self-control … Looking back, it was my own strong motivation that did it.'

Vicky was driven by stubbornness, a determination to prove she could do it: 'I tried using the patches for the first day but I got a skin allergy, so I used the nicotine chewing gum for the next two or three weeks. They kinda took the psychotic edge off my moods. About two or three days after I stopped, I went out for a pizza with my boyfriend. He lit up a cigarette in front of me, I was so ***** off. I got really angry. Generally though, he was quite supportive, except for smoking in front of me, he did want me to give up. My parents, of course, were hugely supportive, but the main thing that kept me going was the thought "I can prove it to myself and everyone else."'

Dylan and Jackie got through the first weeks with the help of NRT. Dylan: 'I did use the nicotine patches for two weeks. The first week I used the medium strength patches and the second week the mild ones. I did buy one more packet (for the third week) just in case I was craving for some nicotine but didn't use them. By the third week I was married and was on my honeymoon.' Jackie: 'I knew I couldn't do it by myself so I bought patches. Spent a hell of a lot of money which was one thing that determined me to go ahead. But I did find them very good. I knew I couldn't get by without the patches.'

James always kept his reasons for stopping to hand: 'I wrote down three reasons on a card and looked at it several times a day.'

Bridget stopped seeing smokers for a month.

Alison went to a stop smoking group and used nicotine gum. 'The group gave me a plan, and rules to stick to. I felt like we were all keeping to the same rules. We were split up into smaller groups. No-one in my group smoked. I think if they had, I would have probably given in, too. We got rid of all our cigarettes, and they told us to take it very seriously. If we were around people who were smoking we should leave, and once you have one, you've had it. I think I did learn from all the times I'd tried before. I used nicotine gum for about three or four months. It really helped as a substitute for the cigarettes. If I was around people who were smoking I'd either leave or chew the gum.'

Sylvia stopped by going to a group. She wasn't suffering any particular health problems at the time, but just thought it was time to stop. After a few days she still had not stopped, and did not like it when the group leader questioned her commitment. For Sylvia being challenged really made the difference. 'The course was run over two weeks, with the first five sessions Monday to Friday of the first week and one follow-up session in the second week. By Wednesday quite a lot of people in the group had stopped. I was still smoking a bit and the group leader was asking me about that. Actually I think he was a bit annoyed with me. I think he thought I was not serious. Later I realized that he was right. I hadn't really decided inside my head that I was going to stop. Really I was just messing around, seeing how it went, but not definitely committed to stopping. He asked me what I was going to do and if I intended to stop. I can't remember what I said at the time but I was annoyed and I think what happened is that I realized he was right and that I was just messing around. I'm so stubborn I decided to prove him wrong. I don't think I could have done it if it wasn't really for me deep down, but you could say he challenged me to make up my mind. I guess what he really did was make me look at myself. It was 12 years ago and I haven't smoked since.'

FEELING WORSE, NOT BETTER?

In the first weeks of stopping, it is quite common to experience a physical reaction to stopping and for coughing to get worse. This is what happened to Ian: 'I won't go into details but it wasn't very pleasant the first few months what was being brought up from my lungs.' It is a good sign because it shows that your lungs are improving and working better. What happened while you were smoking was that the smoke was wearing down the cilia, the tiny hairs that line your lungs and actively brush pollution out of the lungs. Tobacco smoke acts like sandpaper and wears them down so that you don't cough as efficiently as you used to. When you stop the cilia grow again and start ejecting muck from the lungs again, which is why you cough more.

KEEPING HEALTHY

Food and weight

Some people put on weight when they stop smoking. This may be for a number of reasons:

- Nicotine reduces feelings of hunger, so you feel hungrier when you stop smoking.
- Food tastes better when you don't smoke, so you eat more.
- A customary cigarette at the end of a meal is replaced by a second helping of food.
- Some people want to eat more sweet things.

In addition, smoking wastes some of the energy in food by blocking absorption in the stomach. So when you give up smoking, you absorb more energy from the same amount of food.

Unless you are overweight there is no reason why you should diet when you first stop smoking. On the other hand, you don't want to overeat. A much better way of avoiding weight gain is to change the kinds of food you eat and the way you cook them:

- Replace fatty foods with low fat foods.
- Eat plenty of fresh fruit, vegetables and beans (low in calories and full of fibre, so they will fill you up without making you fatter). Eat wholemeal bread (same calories as white bread but more filling). Spread the butter or margarine thinly.
- Eat chicken or white fish instead of red meat, sausages and bacon.
- Replace dairy products (also high in fat) with low fat dairy products, including cheeses.
- Try cutting down on sugar in tea or coffee, or replace it with an artificial sweetener.
- Look for diet versions of soft drinks.
- Reduce alcohol consumption (alcohol is high in calories).
- Grill food instead of frying it.

Think positively about food and stopping smoking. Spend the money you save on cigarettes on better quality food. As food will probably taste better, why not try new recipes and foods?

Exercise

Most people will benefit by becoming more active, but this does not have to mean going to the gym four times a week or entering a marathon. It could mean taking up a sport, but it could just mean just walking more, or cycling, or using the stairs instead of taking the lift, or walking to the shops instead of driving. Whatever you do, exercise burns up calories.

You can: use the stairs, walk instead of taking the bus or car on short journeys, use the bike, do more housework and gardening, play with your children. Ideally you should do some exercise regularly, even if it is just a walk round the block, and choose something which can become part of your daily or regular routine. Do not suddenly take up competitive sports like squash until you are fit. If you have a medical condition it is wise to see your doctor before doing anything strenuous.

ONE DAY AT A TIME

It's a cliché, but like many clichés it became one because it expresses a great truth. We can only live one day (or one hour or minute or second) at a time. It's just that sometimes it doesn't feel like it, especially when we are attempting some big task. If you find yourself worrying about the idea of never ever having a cigarette again, try to stop the thought in its tracks. Today is more than enough for you to get through, and today is all you have to get through. Sometimes when I have a horribly busy day ahead I motivate myself to get through it by visualizing the end of the day, when everything is done, and I'm relaxing in front of the television. It works, try it. Make your goal to get through today without smoking, not today and tomorrow, definitely not today and tomorrow and the rest of the week.

STAGE 1

STAGE 2

STAGE 3

STAGE 4

THINKING ABOUT
STOPPING

PREPARING TO
STOP

STOPPING

Stay alert
watch out for
DANGERS

STAYING
STOPPED

You may be pleasantly surprised to find stopping smoking a lot easier than you thought it would be. If so, it's probably because you have prepared so well and made up your mind you are going to succeed. Or you may have sailed through the early weeks on a wave of determination and commitment but be feeling a little tired now. This chapter is for you.

FEELING DOWNHEARTED?

Don't worry if you find that after the initial few weeks you still have to concentrate to stay stopped – this is very common. It may now seem a bit of a drudge after the initial buzz has faded. Others may forget you have stopped and forget to encourage you.

If you do feel a bit like that, take heart. For most people, the withdrawal symptoms are worst at the beginning and improve steadily over time. Staying stopped gets easier as time goes by. All that is happening now is that you are tired.

The solution is to refresh your determination by reminding yourself of your reasons for stopping and your strategy as often as you need to. Carry this book or your notebook around with you. Re-read the book or the sections that most helped you. Bear in mind, that far from giving something up (well, all right, you are giving something up – a dangerous drug addiction) you are giving yourself something fantastic – a new life. The other enemies of success are boredom, complacency, carelessness, tiredness, and old routines (friends who smoke, places that are smoky, alcohol).

BEATING THE ENEMIES OF SUCCESS

Boredom – keep busy

Complacency – you haven't done it yet, stay focused

Carelessness – stay alert, watch out for dangers

Tiredness – stay motivated, remember your reasons, get support

Old routines – avoid them, change them, take precautions, be careful

KEEP REMEMBERING THE BENEFITS

You will not necessarily feel healthier yet, but you will be healthier from day one. Your risk of getting a serious smoking-related disease starts falling straight away, and continues falling the longer you stay stopped. This is true for smokers at any age (although obviously the sooner you stop, the better).

Toby: 'I think I did give up for the health reasons really, when you think that it could knock ten years off your life. Another thing is that I'm nearly 30. I didn't want to be over 30 and still a smoker.'

You may be beginning to realize that stopping smoking has boosted your pride and self esteem. You have achieved something really worthwhile as a result of your own efforts. You have discovered inner strength you didn't realize you had.

ODETTE · 50

'I lost my sister in July, she died of lung cancer. She was a smoker. Of course I was nervous. I'm still suffering from that, but when I think about her I remember her smoking. I won't start again. Now the weight comes on but I take more exercise. It takes time but I prefer to have fat on me than to be smoking. I feel better. I still think about smoking sometimes but when I think about it I remember the advantages, and of course it saves a lot of money. Andre had the same experience as me. He's very happy now. He has beautiful skin. It was grey before and we were coughing together.'

COSTAS · 54

'I used to have colds regularly, and flu and sore throats. Now I don't have any. I've only had one cold since I gave up, and that was a few weeks ago. I couldn't walk upstairs. There are a lot of staircases in the places I work. I just couldn't do it. Now it's plain sailing – no problem. And I can't stand the smell. If I'm with people who are smoking cigarettes, I have to leave the room.'

ALISON · 34

'It probably took me about three–four years to decide I really wanted to give up. It was a mixture of reasons: health, money, and I've got a little boy who's asthmatic. My husband doesn't smoke either, and he hated me smoking. The main reason, though, was my health. When you first start smoking you can't actually feel the negative effects, so you don't really believe the things you hear are true. But when I'd been smoking a while, I could feel the effects when I ran and I'd get bad coughs. When I'd get a cold, I'd notice that it would quickly go to my chest.'

BRIDGET · 50

'I used to comfort myself with chocolate. I used to go to a newsagent when I got off the bus after working. I automatically found myself in the tobacconist and I was on the point of saying 20 Embassy, and I used to say two Mars Bars please. And then of course the weight went on, and I thought "Well I'm not going to let it worry me because I'll deal with that later." Then I started baking. I'd been to night school and I started baking all these wonderful cakes, and of course eating them. It was just a very short phase. It kept me occupied and there was a reward at the end of it, which was like the reward I was missing.'

BRIAN · 30

'I'm fitter. I feel better. I still go to the gym. I notice I can run several miles. Before I couldn't even do one. It's worth sticking it out for the first six months. If you've got that far it's worth continuing. Take it one day at a time. Try and distract yourself. You've got to break the habit – stop associating the cigarette with the cup of coffee, or whatever moment it was you used to have one.'

HOT STOP TIPS

- Don't forget to get as much support as you need. Keep in touch with a fellow stopper, or a friend who has agreed to help you. Ring them up. Look in on them. Ask them to do the same for you if you need it.

- Make sure you now travel in the non-smoking compartment or section of buses and trains.

- Remember that you will not have to change your routines permanently, only long enough to get through the danger period.

- You may be able to resist smoking in difficult situations better by using NRT before you get into the situation. (See **NRT and other aids to stopping**, p. 90.)

- If boredom is a problem, make sure you keep busy.

HOW LONG DOES IT TAKE TO BECOME A NON-SMOKER?

How long is the danger period? There is remarkable agreement among ex-smokers that one month and three months after stopping are milestones. Of course there are exceptions and it is still true, as I said earlier, that the longer you stay off cigarettes, the easier it generally gets.

Bill had been smoking 40 a day for 22 years when he joined my course. He had tried to stop several times before. He stopped through a combination of nicotine gum and determination. When he started the course, he was not sure he could succeed – but he did. He said that one of the main things he kept in his mind was what might happen to him and his family if he did not stop. This is how he described the first two months:

After three weeks: 'When it's really difficult you start thinking of all the reasons why you should smoke. In fact, the further on it gets from when you stopped, the more I forget why I bothered at all.'

But after four weeks he was already feeling better: 'The worst time for wanting a cigarette was when I was relaxing after working very hard for a period. But I wanted to smoke all the time over the first three weeks. When I really wanted a cigarette I just had to tell myself if I have one I will go back to 40 a day and I'm not doing that.'

After eight weeks it was much easier: 'The last two weeks haven't been so bad now and I'm amazed that I've actually gone eight weeks without a cigarette. I've never gone that far before.'

I last heard from him over a year after the course had finished and he was confident of remaining a non-smoker.

NON-SMOKER OR EX-SMOKER?

Why do I use the term 'non-smoker' rather than 'ex-smoker'? Smokers vary greatly as to how confident they feel about staying stopped. Most ex-smokers feel that they dare not touch even one cigarette. The point to remember here is what I stressed in the first chapter. Stopping smoking is a process and you can see from the experience of the ex-smokers in this book how it progesses over time. In the next chapter I will say a little more about that point in the process when you realize that you have made it. This point does come for most people. This comes over very clearly from the ex-smokers we talked to.

WHEN WAS THE TURNING POINT?

'It was a long time, three or four months before I stopped thinking about smoking.' **Sean, 59**

'Three months was a big turning point. I suddenly realized that I was going two or three days without thinking about it.' **Vicky, 24**

'I had a very short fuse and I was very easily upset. Probably for the first month.' **Bridget, 50**

'[after four months] I can now go out to the pubs without a craving for a smoke.' **Dylan, 35**

'In January, two and a half months after stopping.' **Odette, 50**

'The first week was hell. After that it was OK. I felt proud of the fact that I actually stopped smoking.' **Nino, 52**

So when do you move from being a smoker who is not smoking (an ex-smoker) to being a non-smoker? Will you always be an ex-smoker, in danger of relapse, or will you one day be a non-smoker?

It is difficult to say exactly. Some people will remain off cigarettes but never quite think of themselves as non-smokers. This is similar to alcoholics who feel they will always be an alcoholic – just an alcoholic who has stopped drinking. On the other hand most ex-smokers do reach a point when they hardly think about or crave cigarettes at all, except in unusual circumstances. If you hear ex-smokers say things like 'I still crave for cigarettes after five years,' ask them to describe much more precisely what they feel. You'll probably find they are describing an occasional desire for a cigarette rather than an unbearable craving. It is also something they are able to cope with very easily. Graham describes this very clearly.

GRAHAM · 36

'I also stopped going to pubs for about three months. It took about that time for the intense daily cravings to go away. I still sometimes feel like a fag, I'm not the sort of person who smokes more when I'm stressed out – it's a social thing. The first time I went in a pub it was quite difficult, but I was so set in my mind that I wasn't going to smoke and I'd definitely noticed that I had more money in my pocket. That was a good advantage to stopping. I occasionally get cravings when I see other people smoking now, but it's just a fleeting thought.'

AFTER ALL YOU'VE BEEN THROUGH

A lot of things keep smokers going through the first few months. Pride and stubbornness feature strongly, with the idea that it would be appalling to waste all the hard work that had gone into stopping. Dylan found that he could get through the temptation to smoke by reminding himself what he has achieved: 'The way I deal with any cravings that I have now is to remind myself that if I could go through a wedding without a smoke, I could go through anything without a smoke.' Odette, Louise and Sue knew they had achieved something really major and couldn't bear the thought of having to go through it all again.

ODETTE · 50

'In January, two and a half months after stopping, I went to California for training. In California nobody smokes. It is very hard for a smoker. It was a very, very stressful time for me. The Americans work like crazy. After the second day I was so desperate I found I was thinking about smoking. When I left Montreal I had put on the last patch, so I had nothing left. So on the second day I came back to the hotel and there was a big, big ashtray on a table outside my room full of cigarette butts. I said to myself "I should grab one" but I didn't take one. I thought "I didn't make all this effort just to start again."'

LOUISE · 40

'I was tempted over the first few months but every time I thought about smoking, I thought I couldn't bear to waste all the effort I had put into stopping. You have to understand what is going on in your head ... when I want a cigarette I think "but wouldn't it be awful to go through all that again" ... for one cigarette it's just not worth it.'

> ## SUE · 40
>
> 'It was very hard. Difficult moments? Going out for a drink, or after a meal, it was like a craving, in the pub or anywhere like that. It was bloody-mindedness. If you've given up for 24 hours you've already made a huge sacrifice. Every 24 hours more you survive, you're not going to go through that again.'

GAMES PEOPLE PLAY

This section may not be for you. If you have got this far, you will be very aware of why you want to stop, what the common pitfalls are, and how to avoid them. But then again, perhaps you are still exploring your feelings about smoking or have stopped, but are still not 100 per cent sure why, or if you are doing it for yourself. If so, read on.

Some people reach a point when they have been off cigarettes long enough to feel confident of staying off, and decide to prove they have kicked the habit by having just one. I don't need to tell you if this is a good idea or not, do I? This is probably not you, but you may have tried it in the past or know someone else who tried it. What happened to them? One thing which shows just how addictive smoking is, is the speed with which people go from one cigarette back to their daily consumption before they stopped.

It seems that for most smokers the brain somehow 'remembers' how much nicotine it used to get when it was still smoking; it always stays on the same setting. Even if the first cigarette makes you feel dizzy, the old level of smoking will be re-established quite quickly. So the real question here is not 'Is it all right to have an occasional

SPENCER · 25

'Finally, just before my exams, I started again. I don't know why but it just seemed the correct thing to do. I was stressed, it was late at night, I needed to concentrate and therefore I needed to smoke. So I was back up to 20 a day from that point. From giving up at school I had started smoking at University barely a year and a half later.'

cigarette?' because the vast majority of ex-smokers are absolutely clear, from their own experience, that it is not. The real question is 'Why do some smokers try this?' Are they really trying to prove that they have kicked smoking for good and are in control? I don't think so. I think they are actually smokers who were not ready to stop, but went through it anyway, maybe because of pressure from outside – partner, family, children, friends, doctor. They probably knew they ought to stop but still had not been through the process I explain in the first two chapters of this book. They had not made stopping their decision.

It may sound a bit odd but many smokers go through this process of stopping for someone or something else rather than themselves. It brings us back to one of the commonest (and truest) clichés, that to stop smoking you have really got to want to. Now we can see what these smokers are really doing. They are playing games, because deep down they do not want to stop. Remember Rollo May, the American psychologist, who said that if people really want to do something the possibilities are endless? The opposite is also true. On the whole, if people don't want to do something, they will not.

I came across a curious game years ago in a stop smoking group I was running at the Maudsley Smokers Clinic. A 35-year-old man, Gerald, had, after a few weeks of the course, cut out all his cigarettes – except one. At the end of each day he 'rewarded' himself for not smoking by having a cigarette. OK, you may think, if this is how he eventually went on to stop, then why not? However, after this had gone on for several weeks I asked him: 'If a cigarette is your reward for not smoking how are you going to cut out that one?' He had no idea. It was also undermining the efforts of the other members of the group, who decided that he was not serious about stopping and had actually started getting irritated with him.

He didn't stop. I don't think he came to the course to stop smoking, although part of him may genuinely have wanted to. I suspect that for him the group was also somewhere he could find company, and perhaps an audience? Whatever Gerald's motives were, his strategy of a cigarette at the end of each day as a reward for abstinence was not a strategy. It was a game.

TIME FOR REFLECTION

At the end of each day spend a few quiet minutes to congratulate yourself and remind yourself what you have just achieved. You have got through a day without cigarettes, and lived another day of a life that will get healthier (and richer) from now on.

You should still be trying to live one day at a time. There may be times when you feel overwhelmed by the idea of never having a cigarette again. This will pass, but until it does your best solution is still to concentrate on now, rather than on the next few days, weeks, or months. There is no contradiction in planning ahead but then also living each moment as it happens. Continue applying the basic principles described in this book. Stick to your plan. Continue anticipating problems and make plans to deal with them. Get as much support as you need. Use the checklist to reflect on how the first month went and see if you need to make any adjustments to your plan. After one month the money you didn't spend on tobacco will buy you something you deserve. Reward yourself.

DURING THE FIRST MONTH

The best thing about the month has been …

_____

_____

_____

The biggest problems have been …

_____

_____

_____

How well did I cope?

_____

_____

_____

What adjustments do I need to plan over the next few weeks?

_____

_____

_____

My reward for getting through the first month is …

_____

_____

_____

COMMONLY ASKED QUESTIONS

Where have all the ex-smokers gone?

You know how sometimes when you are trying to do something, you suddenly notice things that are the opposite or that make it more difficult? For example, you want a number 12 bus and so the next four that come along are 36. Or when you decide to give up chocolate for a while, all the adverts on television are for chocolate. The same thing sometimes happens to people who are stopping smoking. They suddenly find that everyone they talk to tried to stop once but relapsed. The successful ex-smokers have mysteriously disappeared. Where to? What is going on?

What is going on is that we perceive things differently. Measured over a long enough period, the frequency of number 36 buses is actually the same as normal, but because we are looking for 12s, we notice the 36s more. But why do ex-smokers notice those who went back to smoking? Where did all the other ex-smokers go? You are probably only noticing the lapsed smokers because subconsciously the part of you that wants to continue smoking is looking for them. What this really reflects is the old conflict within you. The conflict is between the you that wants to stop smoking and the you that wants to go back to smoking. Stamp on the old you. It's trying to pull a dirty trick. Of course, because you have prepared so well, you will have already dealt with this conflict, so it should be easy now.

What if I slip up?

If you slip up, treat it as that, a slip up not a failure. It's not the end of the world. Stopping smoking is a process, and most smokers try several times before eventually succeeding. The chances are that you probably have already stopped and then gone back to smoking before. Each time this happens you can learn from it. If necessary, have a few days' or weeks' break until you have enough energy and determination to stop again. Don't worry about it, absolutely don't feel guilty, and continue your journey to non-smoking tomorrow. If it helps, write down what you learned so that you are better prepared next time.

MARION · 39

'The worst time was at the beginning. Then, when I felt I wanted a cigarette people around me said "Don't. You've done so well." But I still have that feeling sometimes. When I lapsed, only twice ever, it wasn't difficult to stop at one. But I think it's difficult when you're under stress and you have one, then another. I wasn't under stress when I had one, I was with friends and I was relaxed, it didn't wake up a craving. It's dangerous to have more than one because you might go back. Once you've been a smoker it's always there.'

BEAR THIS IN MIND...

What is worth remembering is that in most countries smokers are a minority, and in many, a minority that is getting smaller. The rights of non-smokers (not to be forced to breathe in other people's tobacco smoke) are gradually being recognized. More and more public places, including restaurants, cinemas, and work places, are introducing restrictions and divisions that provide clean air for those who want it. Which is making it easier for smokers who want to stop.

FREE AT LAST!

While there is a lot we still don't know about tobacco smoke and what is in it, we do know that when you stop smoking two things happen: you break your physical addiction to smoking and you get rid of the habit. One process is physical, the other mental. Just as it may take three months for some of the chemical changes that occur when you stop to take place, the psychological change takes time as well.

ENJOYING SUCCESS

The psychological process is similar in some ways to bereavement or getting over a broken relationship. Ex-smokers often describe it like this, talking about missing cigarettes, constantly thinking about them, wishing to go back to them. In fact, one famous advertising campaign presented cigarettes in this way, as a faithful companion: 'You're never alone with a Lucky.' The good thing is that as with broken relationships, even if it takes time, a day comes when we realize we have got over it. At first, you feel down, flat, depressed. Then one day, you wake up feeling noticeably more cheerful, and gradually realize that yesterday you went through the whole day without thinking about cigarettes. That is often the first sign that you are changing and that you are no longer at serious risk.

There will also come a time when you are not at risk at all any more. Clearly this is psychological. Your mind slowly gets used to the fact that you are no longer smoking. It adjusts to the change in your behaviour. You may not be aware of it, but you have become a non-smoker. Your normal habits and reactions, routines and mannerisms, become those of a non-smoker. And somehow your self-image changes. When does this happen? At different times for different people. But it does happen and when it does you will feel it.

When it does, give yourself time to be aware of what you have achieved, to enjoy it, and to congratulate yourself for it. Some of the smokers we talked to described stopping as the most difficult thing they did, and the greatest thing they did. In terms of how incredibly dangerous smoking is, you are unlikely to do anything else in your life, ever, that will have such an impact on your health. Ex-smokers quite often decide, when this has sunk in, to make other changes in their life, and this could be a good time. You have proved you do have willpower, you have conquered one of the strongest addictions, you can do anything you want.

If you did put on weight while you were stopping and sensibly waited to tackle it, now could be the time. For David (see p. 88) stopping smoking was part of a process that changed his whole life, and although I never saw her again, I hope Greta (see p. 24) was also able to go on from stopping smoking to deal with other things. This could be a good time to look at other parts of your life. Stopping smoking could be the beginning of a new life. I am going to leave the last word with the ex-smokers.

A NEW LIFE

'Giving up smoking was the most traumatic thing in my life. I haven't touched a cigarette since, as I could never go through giving up again. I couldn't talk on the phone or drink a cup of coffee and I was in bed at 8 o'clock every night for the first fortnight. I just didn't feel I could relax. In a way I felt worse off, for a period anyway. But now I'm so glad that I've given up. It's so anti-social. It's an awful stigma to have. People don't really smoke in other people's houses any more, and what pleasure can you get out of standing on the doorstep every time you want a cigarette? I'm very, very glad that I've given up. I'd feel like I was being cast aside by society if I still smoked. When I was young it was such a fashionable thing to smoke, but now it's quite the opposite.' **Eirlys, 62**

'The other thing that you might be interested in knowing is that I started taking vitamins at about the same time, for my health, and have continued taking them ever since. It's almost as if during my adolescence and during my 20s, I wasn't particularly interested in my health, but changed my attitudes when I hit 30.' **James, 48**

'Yes, I was tempted, but I never touched one. It is over two years now. I never touched a cigarette. And occasionally even now when I see somebody smoking I say maybe I should smoke a cigarette because I really enjoyed it. It is one of the most difficult things you can do. Very hard. But the rewards are good, you can smell better, everything smells better. I'm proud of the fact that I did it.' **Nino, 52**

'I don't really have urges to smoke any more, in fact there's a total aversion by now. Walking into a room where people are smoking, it turns on me, makes me feel rather nauseous. In a confined space, like a car, I don't think that I could stomach someone smoking next to me. It took a good twelve months for me to reach that stage.' **Robin, 61**

'I'm fitter. I feel better. I still go to the gym. I notice I can run several miles. Before I couldn't even do one … My wife said a few weeks ago: "You don't realize that now, after an evening with friends, they get up and for a few minutes they're coughing and wheezing, but you're not doing it any more."' **Brian, 30**

'After about a year I could go a whole week without thinking about smoking, and now I can go at least a month. I feel so much healthier, and very positive about being in control of my life. I was able to do it and I feel so proud of myself. I also think I've got a lot more respect for my health – when I used to smoke I'd think "what's the point of going to the gym, I'm already ****ing my body up". Now I go to the gym regularly, on average about two times a week. I also eat more healthily. Food has always tasted good but now it tastes even better. I have put on weight, about half a stone, but I was a bit skinny before, so I'm probably a much healthier weight now. I used to get colds every winter, about four each winter. Now it's unusual if I even get one. Also my clothes don't smell any more, that's kinda nice too. Yeah, after about three months it got easier, but it was quite a long time after

I stopped, probably about a year or so, that I realized that I'd gone for long periods of time, weeks, without even thinking about having a cigarette. That was when I knew I was finally free. I thought "God, I'm really over it." I really started training, I wanted to do a marathon and still would like to. There's no way I would have even thought to do that if there was a risk of me smoking again.' **Vicky, 24**

'I definitely feel a lot healthier. I used to have a really bad smoker's cough and now I have no problems with my chest at all. That's one thing. The freedom is another, not having anything controlling your life. You don't realize how it controls you when you're smoking, not until you stop. Also with the children, I used to feel so guilty. Now I don't have all those feelings of guilt, that I'm doing them harm. I also used to worry about cancer. When you smoke, you feel like your life won't be as good without it, in fact it's so much better. You think you'll never get over wanting a cigarette, but you do and your life feels so much better without them.' **Alison, 34**

'I occasionally get cravings when I see other people smoking now, but it's just a fleeting thought. After about a year and a half I considered myself to be a non-smoker. I've put on half a stone since I stopped smoking, but I'm going to persevere with that. I just think sod it, I feel so much healthier. I play five-a-side football and I used to feel wheezy at the end of any game, now I don't.' **Graham, 36**

David was a senior civil servant in his mid-fifties with a high-pressure job. When he first came to see me he looked grey. He needed heart bypass surgery and had been referred to our clinic by the surgeon, who told him that he must stop smoking before he would operate, otherwise the surgery wouldn't work. He came to see me at the Maudsley Smokers Clinic and during our first talk he asked me directly: 'If I don't stop will you tell the surgeon?' I don't remember all the details of the conversation but my answer was 'yes', and my reason was that if I agreed I would not tell, then that might undermine his attempt to stop. He wanted to stop but was not convinced he could. But he had a pretty strong motivation to stop now. He came to the group and he stopped, but he did a lot more than stop. He had been thinking about his life anyway, prompted partly by his condition, and had been wondering if he wanted to continue his job. Stopping smoking and the operation triggered change. One year later, he had resigned, enrolled in a course on anthropology, which he had been interested in for years, was visibly happier and contented – and pinker! He looked healthy again. For David, stopping smoking really was the beginning of a new life.

NRT AND OTHER AIDS TO STOPPING

You don't have to go it alone. As well as the information and guidance in this book, there are treatments and other types of support that can help you when you stop smoking. Here is some information on the best known.

NICOTINE REPLACEMENT THERAPY

Nicotine replacement therapy (NRT) has probably saved millions of lives worldwide already. It is very useful when people are stopping smoking because it reduces the nicotine withdrawal symptoms. It is also the best researched of all the aids to stopping.

Who invented NRT?

On December 12, 1967, Dr Claes Lundgren of Lund University in Sweden wrote to a friend in charge of research at the Swedish pharmaceutical company AB Leo, suggesting the idea for a tobacco substitute. Lundgren had noticed that submarine crews, who were not allowed to smoke, were able to satisfy their craving by chewing tobacco instead. Lundgren's friend Ove Ferno immediately saw the potential of the idea. He had become a heavy smoker in the Second World War but one day, when he ran out of tobacco, had tried the only tobacco he could get hold of – herbal tobacco. He did not find it satisfying and realized it was because it had no nicotine in it.

When Ove Ferno received Claes Lundgren's letter he realized that a tobacco substitute could help smokers stop, and that a product that could do that could help millions of smokers. Ferno and his research department then developed the first product, nicotine chewing gum, which received its first product licence in 1978 in Switzerland. The first scientific study which proved the gum worked, published by a London team led by Dr Michael Russell, appeared in the *British Medical Journal* in 1982. Since then many companies have moved into the field and many more products developed so that we no longer talk about nicotine chewing gum but about nicotine replacement therapy, or NRT for short.

What is NRT?

There are currently six different types of NRT products, although they are not all available in every country yet. The products are nicotine gum, patches, nasal spray, inhalators, tablets and lozenges. They all have one thing in common: they allow the user to get nicotine into the body but without the poisonous chemicals contained in tobacco smoke (see **More facts about smoking**, p. 101). In other words, they allow you to get a 'clean' source of nicotine while you are getting over the withdrawal symptoms. This way you break the process of stopping smoking into two stages: first getting used to becoming a non-smoker, then gradually withdrawing from the nicotine. All the products contain nicotine, which is absorbed in the mouth (by chewing the gum, dissolving the tablet under the tongue, sucking the lozenge, sucking on the inhaler), the nose (the nasal spray is sprayed into the nose), or through the skin (the patch).

Does it work?

Yes. But it is not a magic cure. In fact, there are no magic cures to stop smoking. If there were, you would not be reading this book, and a multi-millionaire would be relaxing somewhere in the sun enjoying the profits of his or her genius. I will say a little more about this later on, because there are 'treatments' around that claim amazingly high success rates. But when you look carefully into the small print you find that their figures are not quite what they led you to believe.

But to get back to NRT. It roughly doubles your chance of stopping smoking, compared with if you don't use it. This is a very impressive result. It is important to remember also that this figure is not based on the exaggerated claims of a marketing department or an enthusiast selling their own product. This figure is based on research conducted by independent scientists and doctors all over the world, over more than 20 years, in almost a hundred published scientific articles. In other words it is not a fluke result but one which has stood the test of time.

However, you must use NRT properly. Read the instructions in the pack carefully, and ideally discuss it with a pharmacist when you buy it. As each product has slightly different characteristics and each smoker is different, you will probably need advice on how to decide which product is best for you.

For how long should I use NRT?

For as long as you feel you need it and as long as it is helping you. Most smokers use too little rather than too much, because they think that it is addictive, unsafe or too expensive. In fact, it is much less addictive and much safer than cigarettes. Once you have stopped smoking and are confident of staying stopped, then you cut out the NRT. Ideally, you should use NRT as a substitute for smoking, and not smoke as well as use NRT. There is no evidence that it is harmful to smoke and use NRT at the same time but there is no point. NRT will help you stop if you want to and if you make an effort. But if you are not trying to stop it cannot help.

If you have already tried NRT in the past, and you did not succeed in stopping, don't worry, and don't blame the NRT. There may have been other reasons why you couldn't stop that time and when you are ready, you can try again.

It is important to accept that NRT isn't a magic cure for smoking, because it will not exactly reproduce the effect you get from smoking. As I said in Stage 2, inhaled tobacco smoke results in nicotine reaching the brain incredibly quickly – in around seven seconds. The addictiveness of smoking is linked to the simplicity of the behaviour (lighting up, holding the cigarette to the mouth, breathing in) and the quick drug fix. NRT does not get nicotine into the blood as quickly. This is why it is not as addictive as smoking and not as satisfying. You must really want to stop.

Is it safe?

The top world experts agree that NRT is safe when used correctly, and that it is much safer than smoking. It is safe to use as much as you need to because it is quite difficult to overdose on it. If you did, the worst that is likely to happen is that you would feel sick. However, at the moment most NRT products are not recommended for pregnant women or people under 18. If you suffer from a medical condition or are taking medication, you should also seek advice from your doctor or pharmacist. If you have any doubts at all, ask their advice.

Research is continuing to find out if nicotine can be harmful. It is possible that it may have a small effect on heart and vascular disease, but so far there is no evidence it causes cancer. The key thing to remember here is that even if it turned out that nicotine could be harmful, you are getting nicotine in much smaller doses than from smoking anyway, and only using NRT for a short time while you are stopping.

Is it addictive?

Nicotine is addictive, which is why so many smokers find it so difficult to stop, but it's also why NRT is so helpful. Most people find it easy to come off NRT after a few weeks or months as it contains less nicotine than tobacco and, therefore, is nothing like as addictive. A few do continue using it for a long time, but there is no evidence that this is harmful, and if in the longer term this helps them stop smoking for good, then it is well worthwhile.

How do I choose which product is best for me?

All six NRT products have similar success rates, so depending on availability, you should choose the one that suits you best on practical grounds. It may be a matter of trial and error, but your pharmacist should be able to give helpful advice. If you are allergic to nicotine or plasters, ask for advice.

The **patch** is discreet and easy to use. It is put on each morning, is designed to be worn for 16 or 24 hours, and comes in different doses. If you smoke 10 cigarettes a day or more you should normally start with the highest dose patch.

The **gum** allows good control of nicotine dose (when your craving is strong, chew quickly) and comes in 2mg or 4mg doses and in different flavours. The taste can be unpleasant at first but most people get used to it in a week or so. It is important to chew slowly to get the most out of the gum because any nicotine that is swallowed is wasted. The nicotine is absorbed through the lining of the mouth. If you smoke more than 20 a day you should try the stronger gum.

The **spray** is for very addicted smokers. It consists of a small bottle of nicotine solution. When the top is pressed down it delivers a dose of nicotine in a spray. Nicotine is absorbed faster than from other forms of NRT, and this can be better for heavier smokers. However it can be difficult to get used to because the spray can irritate the nose. Smokers who still experience severe craving and withdrawal with the other NRT products should try the nasal spray. (In Britain at the moment the spray is only available on prescription.)

The **inhalator** can be good if you miss the ritual of smoking. It consists of a plastic mouthpiece and a supply of replaceable nicotine cartridges that fit inside it. You draw on it like a cigarette. Despite its name the nicotine does not reach the lungs, but stops in the mouth and throat. Like the gum, tablet and lozenge, the inhalator delivers nicotine through the lining of the mouth.

The **tablet** is discreet and flexible and gives good control of the nicotine dose. It is a small tablet which you place under the tongue. You do not chew or swallow it. It works like the gum in allowing nicotine to be absorbed through the lining of the mouth.

The **lozenge** is the newest of these products and works like the gum and tablet. The manufacturers do not recommend it for heavier smokers (more than 20 a day).

WHERE CAN YOU BUY NRT?

Most NRT products are available over the counter from pharmacists. Some are sold in supermarkets and ordinary shops and are not restricted to pharmacies. In countries where cigarettes are expensive, like Britain for example, a full course of treatment comes out a little cheaper than smoking. But in countries where cigarettes are cheap these products will be very expensive for smokers. In Britain, unfortunately, they are not generally available on prescription from the National Health Service (NHS).

If you usually wake up with a strong craving to smoke and have your first cigarette within half an hour of waking, then you should either try taking an NRT product immediately on waking, which you might find unpalatable, or use the 24-hour patch. This will make sure that your body still has some nicotine in it when you wake which will take the edge off the craving.

NON-NICOTINE DRUGS

Several non-nicotine drugs are being researched to see if they might help smokers stop. One that has been shown to be effective is a drug called bupropion which you can only get on prescription from your doctor. This is an anti-depressant which was discovered to have an effect on smoking by accident. Scientists do not know why, but it has been shown in research trials to help smokers stop just as effectively as NRT. However, these are early days yet and only a few research

A QUICK GUIDE TO NRT

NRT can help you stop even if you have tried it before.

Clinical trials show that if you want to stop smoking **NRT doubles your chance of success**.

NRT is not a magic cure. It does not provide a complete replacement for cigarettes, nor replace the need for willpower. But when you stop, it will help with the craving and withdrawal.

NRT usually provides nicotine in a way which **is** slower and less satisfying, but **safer and less addictive than cigarettes**.

Although **NRT** provides nicotine it **does not contain tar and carbon monoxide** as tobacco smoke does. There is no evidence that nicotine causes cancer.

NRT reduces withdrawal symptoms like irritability, depression and craving, although it does not get rid of them entirely.

Very few people become addicted to NRT. Some ex-smokers continue to use it for a year or more but this is usually because of concern about returning to smoking.

For the best results **NRT should be used in sufficient quantities and for long enough**. You should follow the instructions in the pack, and seek advice from the pharmacist if you need more information.

trials have been published so far. It does have one potential advantage over NRT: because it does not contain nicotine it may be suitable for pregnant smokers.

Bupropion is already licenced for use in some countries, for example the USA, Canada, Mexico and Brazil. Licence applications have been made in Europe and it is expected that the drug (under the brand name Zyban), will come onto the market in Europe during 2000.

HYPNOSIS AND ACUPUNCTURE

These therapies are popular with smokers but there is no scientific evidence that they work. One reason for this is that they are difficult to study using traditional research methods. For example, there is no agreed definition of what 'hypnosis' is. If you don't know what something is, you cannot easily study it scientifically. However, many treatments work not because they have a specific effect but because they boost a person's motivation. Anything can do this if you believe in it. This is sometimes called the 'placebo effect'.

If you want to try such treatments, choose practitioners who are registered with some official, national association. This should give you at least some protection and indicate that they practise in a professional way. As for what they offer, you must pay the fee and make up your own mind. If you believe in the treatment or in the person offering it, you cannot see any disadvantages, and you can afford it, then go for it.

This advice applies to any treatment, such as laser therapy, for which there is no scientific proof that it works.

BEWARE EXAGGERATED CLAIMS

I recently read a headline in a newspaper: 'Miracle herbs to help you stop smoking.' It went on to say that the therapy 'claims a 70 per cent success rate' and cost £100 (US$ 150). The problem with most of these claims is that they don't explain how they arrived at the figure. I can tell you from more than 25 years of helping smokers stop, that there is no such thing as a 70 per cent success rate with smokers – defined the way scientific researchers define success. For example, in most NRT studies the results are given one year after treatment. In this article I read that the creators of the herb said that 'in a trial two-thirds of people stopped smoking after seven days.' Seven days is very different from one year. A lot of people will go back to smoking during that year, as you know from your past experience, so the real success rate will be much lower than the claimed 70 per cent. And as you also know from your experience, there are no miracle cures, except the miracle of willpower.

Unfortunately, such exaggerated claims are common and they are sometimes accompanied by claims that this is 'the' way to stop smoking, or 'the only way to stop'! As I said at the beginning of the book, the way to stop smoking is the way that works for you. Not too much can be done to stop people making these claims, but if you are interested in one of these commercial treatments, or privately run stop smoking groups or courses – and you value your money – ask them a few questions first:

- Are your success rates calculated after one year?
- Did you count all the people you could not contact at one year as still smoking?
- Did you take account of smokers who would have stopped without the treatment anyway, and deduct them from your figures?

I'm sorry to say that you will probably not get clear answers to these questions. Remember also that treatments that are expensive will tend to attract smokers who are very motivated to stop, and that these are more likely to succeed.

STOP SMOKING GROUPS

There may be publicly- or privately-run stop smoking groups near where you live, or at your workplace. In some countries, Britain for example, there is now a national policy on helping smokers stop, and the NHS is developing services for this. These services include groups. If you want help and support from a group run as part of the health service, then ask your doctor, nurse or pharmacist where the nearest group is, and if that fails find the name of your health authority in the phone book and ask them. If you don't know the name, ask directory enquiries.

These groups work. They are not miracle cures, but they offer encouragement and support for smokers who need it. David, Alison, and Doreen all went to stop smoking groups run free as part of the NHS, while Greta and Sylvia went to groups which I ran at their workplace.

A well-run group will offer you support, advice and expert information from a trained specialist. However, such groups are still not common.

ALISON · 34

'I decided to try again when I saw an advert for a group. I thought that giving up with other people might help me break it. I went to that and it really helped, being with other people who are in the same boat got me through the hard times. It also helped because I was aiming at a week at a time. When I'd tried before, I'd be thinking about never having a cigarette again for the rest of my life.'

TELEPHONE HELPLINES

The following telephone helplines are available.

UK: Department of Health   0800 169 0 169
UK: Quitline   0800 00 22 00 (Also runs Bengali, Gujarati, Hindi, Punjabi, Urdu, Turkish and Kurdish quitlines and a quitline for pregnant women)
Scotland: Smokeline   0800 84 84 84
Wales: Smokers' helpline   0345 69 75 00
Northern Ireland: the Ulster Cancer Foundation will send an advice kit . Ring   028 9066 3281
Republic of Ireland: Quitline   0850 201 203
Australia: Quitline   131848

If you live in a country where there is a lot of anti-smoking activity there are likely to be free or cheap telephone helplines. These are often staffed by well-trained counsellors and provide valuable support when it is convenient for you.

GET SUPPORT

I want to repeat the advice I gave earlier in the book. If you need support find it. A pharmacist may be able to help, or your doctor or nurse, but don't underestimate the value of friends, family, or colleagues.

Finally, you might remember Marion who said how much it helps in this country that smoking is less common in public (she comes from Spain). If you find it unpleasant to be forced to breathe other people's second-hand tobacco smoke, say so politely but clearly. Stand up for your right to clean air. Remember that non-smokers are in the majority and so providing smoke-free spaces, in restaurants for example, ought to reflect that fact.

MORE FACTS ABOUT SMOKING

THE LINK BETWEEN SMOKING AND LUNG CANCER

The link between smoking and lung cancer was unexpectedly discovered in the 1940s and 1950s. Professor Sir Richard Doll, the British scientist who published his conclusions on lung cancer in 1950, says that scientists expected the increase in lung cancer to be connected to the increase in road traffic. This was because they knew that tar could cause cancer, and tar was used in road building. They were surprised when they discovered that it wasn't the road building or increase in traffic that was correlated with lung cancer but smoking.

In the USA the discovery was also a surprise. In 1919, Dr Alton Ochsner was a medical student at Washington University. At that time, lung cancer was so rare that his professor called all the medical students round to see a patient who had it. He told them that they would never see another case in their careers. Ochsner was astonished when 17 years later in 1936, he saw six patients with lung cancer in six months. He couldn't quite believe it and so looked into their backgrounds. He found that all had started smoking during the First World War, all were men and all were heavy smokers. He also discovered that smoking in the USA was very rare before the First World War, but much commoner by the end.

Over the next 10 years medical authorities were alerted to the problem and in Britain and America large-scale research studies were begun. Sir Richard Doll began what became known as the British Doctors Study. They did a survey of doctors and followed them through their lifetime. In fact the study continues to this day, taken over by Doll's colleague Richard Peto (now Sir Richard) and it was this study, along with an American study, that confirmed that smoking causes lung cancer.

Doll's work has been continued by Richard Peto and the British Doctors Study has so far followed its subjects for more than 40 years. Peto is probably the world's best-known and highly respected epidemiologist now and is studying the emergence of lung cancer in countries that took up smoking much later. It is sad that while smoking is going down in developed countries, it is increasing in the developing world, and Peto estimates that in the twenty-first century, more than 900 million people will be killed by smoking.

JUST HOW DANGEROUS IS SMOKING?

If you take up smoking in your teens, which is when most people take it up, and smoke throughout your life, then you are 20 times more likely to die from lung cancer than a lifelong non-smoker is. This is such a huge risk that other factors like diet and exercise hardly affect it at all. When we consider the risk from all diseases, it is huge. One in four smokers will die in middle age as a result of smoking, and a further one in four will die in old age because of their smoking. You might be pleased to know, incidentally, that scientists define middle age as 35–69.

Unfortunately, smoking also causes other diseases, including coronary heart disease, bronchitis and emphysema (chronic lung disease), strokes, cancer of the mouth, oesophagus, larynx, bladder, kidney and pancreas, peripheral vascular disease, and peptic ulcer. In Britain about 90 per cent of all lung cancer and emphysema is caused by smoking, and about 20 per cent of coronary heart disease. Professor Peto's conclusion is that 'HIV and tobacco are the only two major causes of death that are increasing substantially throughout the world.' And in terms of overall deaths, HIV does not yet come remotely close to tobacco.

IS IT WORTH STOPPING?

Yes. Scientists can't yet predict which smokers will get smoking-related diseases and which will not, so the only safe way to avoid this risk is to stop smoking altogether. Health begins to improve immediately on stopping – irrespective of age. Within days of stopping, the heart will beat about ten beats per minute less, and each heartbeat will deliver more oxygen to the rest of the body. Blood pressure falls and circulation starts improving in as little as one hour. The lungs start to clear out mucus and other pollutants during the first day, and within the first week the bronchial passages begin to clear and breathing becomes easier. Circulation improves in weeks and the excess risk of serious heart disease is halved in the first year of stopping. At about ten years the risk of a heart attack falls to about the same as someone who has never smoked.

WHY IS SMOKING SO DANGEROUS?

Smoking is dangerous because when tobacco burns, thousands of chemicals are vaporized and inhaled into your lungs. Some of these chemicals you would get just from burning vegetable matter – leaves – of any kind. It is possible that if you stood downwind of a bonfire for 40 years and inhaled the smoke, that would be dangerous, too. But as you know from trying to avoid bonfire smoke when it chases you round the fire, you cannot breathe it in, because it makes you choke. Tobacco smoke is different because, as I explained earlier in the book, cigarettes are carefully engineered so that the smoke is 'palatable' and goes down easily. Earlier in the twentieth century the tobacco smoked was stronger, rougher and more difficult to inhale. It is only over the last few decades that the tobacco industry has 'refined' the product to make it easier to use. They have done this quite deliberately by

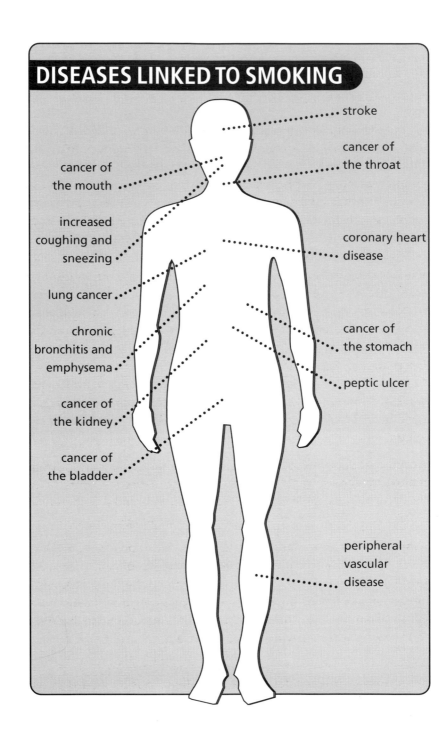

DISEASES LINKED TO SMOKING

stroke

cancer of the throat

cancer of the mouth

increased coughing and sneezing

coronary heart disease

lung cancer

chronic bronchitis and emphysema

cancer of the stomach

peptic ulcer

cancer of the kidney

cancer of the bladder

peripheral vascular disease

using additives such as flavouring agents (and we don't know what else because they haven't told us yet). It is this cocktail of chemicals, burned at about 1000 degrees celsius and then inhaled, which is so toxic.

In a BBC documentary series called *Tobacco Wars*, first shown in 1999, former industry executives talked about this engineering of the product. A former director of applied research with one of the tobacco companies said: 'The phenomenal success of the cigarette is based on how easy it is to inhale nicotine compared to the cigars or pipes that were used in the last century. The modern cigarette is extremely complex. It contains everything from sugar to liquorice, chocolate, herbs and spices. There are 8000 or more chemicals that come out when you light it and having them delivered in the right ratios is a substantial engineering feat.'

Now you can see why the ingredients of tobacco smoke are not printed on the packet. So here are just a few, gleaned from the investigations of the Ministry of Health in British Columbia, the International Agency for Research on Cancer and the US Surgeon General. They are found in tiny quantities. Some are used for flavour, some are there to make the nicotine absorption more efficient, and the others? Well, who knows? Perhaps the tobacco industry should tell us.

Acetone Acetone is a component of most paint strippers and varnish removers. High concentrations can cause you to become dizzy, light-headed and pass out. It can irritate the eyes, nose and throat and can affect you when breathed in and by passing through your skin.

Ammonia This is produced by rotting and decomposing animal and vegetable matter. It is used in making fertilizer, plastics, dyes and textiles. Prolonged exposure to its vapour can be fatal. Breathing ammonia may irritate the lungs, causing coughing and/or shortness of breath. Higher exposures can cause a build-up of fluid in the lungs (pulmonary oedema), which can cause death.

Arsenic Arsenic is a silver-grey, brittle, crystalline solid. It is a poison often used in insecticides and weed killers. It is also used in the manufacture of some military poison gases. Arsenic is a carcinogen (causes cancer) and may damage a developing foetus.

Benzene A potential carcinogen, exposure can cause you to become dizzy and light-headed. It can also irritate the nose and throat and may cause an upset stomach and vomiting. It is used as a solvent for gums, fats, waxes and resins, in the manufacture of drugs and the production of nylon. It is also found in petrol.

Beryllium Although safe when in a large solid mass, fumes or dust from beryllium are highly toxic. It is a carcinogen and can cause severe bronchitis or pneumonia after high exposure, causing death in severe cases. High or repeated lower exposure can cause scars to develop in the lungs and other body organs. In severe cases, grave disability and heart failure can occur. It is used extensively in manufacturing electrical components, chemicals, ceramics and x-ray tubes.

Cadmium A highly toxic, silver-white metal. The cumulative effects of ingesting cadmium are similar to those of mercury poisoning (see below). It is carcinogenic, can cause malformations in a foetus and reproductive damage. Repeated lower exposures can cause permanent kidney damage, emphysema, anaemia and loss of smell.

DDT An insecticide which is toxic to many animals (including us) and is now banned from use. It tends to accumulate in the ecosystem because it is difficult to break down into non-poisonous substances.

Formaldehyde A highly flammable liquid/gas, it is used as a disinfectant, germicide, fungicide, an embalming fluid and in home insulation and pressed wood products. Recent tests have indicated that it is a carcinogen. It can affect you when inhaled and by passing through skin. Exposure irritates the eyes, nose and throat, and can cause skin and lung allergy.

Hydrogen cyanide Extremely poisonous. Low levels of exposure can irritate the skin, and may cause a rash.

Lead Lead can affect you when breathed in and if swallowed from food, drinks or cigarettes. Low levels can cause tiredness, mood changes, headaches, stomach problems and insomnia. Lead exposure increases the risk of high blood pressure.

Mercury It is used in thermometers, barometers, vapour lamps, mirror coating, and in making chemicals and electrical equipment. Mercury is a corrosive chemical.

Nickel A silver-white, hard metal resistant to corrosion. It is a carcinogen and may damage the developing foetus. Lung allergy occasionally occurs with asthma-type effects. High exposure can cause coughing, shortness of breath and fluid in the lungs. It is used in electroplating and in making coins, batteries, catalysts and metal alloys such as stainless steel.

Selenium A carcinogenic mineral, which has become a major health concern because it increases the risk of lung cancer.

These are just a few, and don't forget that according to a former tobacco industry research director there are 8000 or more. The list includes such exotic names as Acetaldehyde, Butyraldehyde, Cyclohexane, Hydroquinone, Methyl Acrylate, Naphthalene, Nitric oxide, n-Nitrosodimethylamine, Phenol, Polonium-210, Toluene, Vinyl chloride. Aren't you wondering why cigarette packets don't tell you a little more about what you are consuming? I am.

Carbon monoxide and cardiovascular disease

One of the constituents of the tobacco smoke you inhale into your lungs is a colourless, odourless gas called carbon monoxide (CO). It is the same gas that is produced by car exhausts and in high concentrations it is extremely toxic. It passes from your lungs straight into the blood where it is absorbed into your red blood cells, the haemoglobin. It has such a strong chemical affinity with haemoglobin that it displaces oxygen. This means that smokers have blood circulating around their body which is short of oxygen by anything from about 2 per cent up to 15 per cent or, very rarely, even higher. A fairly typical level for a regular smoker would be about 5–10 per cent. This means that your heart has to work harder to pump blood round the body to get enough oxygen to the cells. And the heart is doing this extra work when its own supply of blood, which is part of the same blood system, is short of oxygen. This is one of the factors that contributes to cardiovascular disease in smokers.

Simple machines have been developed, much like the breathalysers for alcohol, which measure your carbon monoxide level. In just a few seconds they measure your CO level, which tells you how much smoke you normally inhale. If you want to check your CO level you will need to ask your doctor or nurse (or possibly pharmacist). While these machines are not widely available at present, they will probably become more common over the next few years.

AND FINALLY, DID THEY KNOW?

A former biochemist at RJ Reynolds was doing research in 1970 which showed a connection between smoking and emphysema. On the BBC's *Tobacco Wars*, he said: 'There was evidence starting to build in our own work that there was a connection. They had demonstrated emphysema in rabbits that had been exposed to cigarette smoke as defined by a clinical pathologist ... I was asked to submit all our laboratory note books ... They contained all our experiments ... our results. The explanation given was that the legal department wanted to see if there was something potentially dangerous to the company.' Later, the scientists were told that the notebooks had been 'accidentally destroyed'. He said 'As a scientist, I was watching two and a half years of hard effort go for nought. It's been a shameful track record. It's been one of deception, cover-up, misleading – intentionally misleading – the public and all in the name of profit.'

ACKNOWLEDGEMENTS

I owe huge thanks to Rachel Hodgson and Carolyn Quillfeldt who conducted most of the interviews with smokers for this book and to Rachel for additional research. Their work has added to the book the voices of the people who really matter in all this, the (ex-)smokers, and we are extremely grateful to them for sharing their experiences with us. Sincere thanks also to my editors Viv Bowler, Martha Caute and Sue Tucker who offered reassurance and support both to me and my prose. I am then grateful for the help people offered, with ideas about the structure of the book, by answering my technical questions, and in other ways, especially Martin Jarvis who offered helpful comments on the manuscript. They were: Clive Bates, Keith Bolling, Karl Brookes, Mark Duman, Adrian Dzialdowski, Debra Gill, Jeff Fowles, Ray Hodgson, Paul Hooper, Richard Peto, Gay Sutherland, Robert West and Stephen Woodward. Finally, thank you to the many smokers I have seen over more than two decades, and from whom I have learned such a lot.

Martin Raw

Notes

Notes

Notes